THE SECOND CRUSADE

Ed Erny

Published by One Mission Society
P. O. Box A, Greenwood, IN 46142

To Bob, Virginia
With love from
Ed Erny

Pictured on front cover, L to R:
Kemp Edwards, Grant Nealis, Lowell Williamson, Hudson Hess,
Ed Erny, Stan Dyer, Helmut Schultz, Austin Boggan

Copyright @ 2012
One Mission Society
Box A, Greenwood, IN 46142

ISBN-978-1-880338-15-5

Ed Erny
The Second Crusade

Printed in the United States of America
by Evangel Press, Nappanee, Indiana

CONTENTS

Chapter		Page

DEDICATION

This book is dedicated to my beloved wife and helpmeet, Rachel. For 50 year her indefatigable labors, typing, proofing, correcting, and encouraging have made possible my books.

FOREWORD

In a previous book entitled *Young Men of the Cross*, I wrote of the vision of OMS founders Charles Cowman and Ernest Kilbourne to literally put the Scriptures and plan of salvation in every home in Japan. This program initially called The Great Village Campaign was begun in 1913 and completed in 1918. To finish the final phase of the campaign, OMS solicited assistance from ten young men, students in God's Bible School where Cowman and Kilbourne had studied prior to coming to Japan.

Following the close of World War II, a call came for another campaign, now labeled the Every Creature Crusade. This was in part a response to General MacArthur's summons to send missionaries to evangelize Japan then recovering from the horrors and shame of the war. In 1952, my father, OMS President Dr. Eugene Erny, sent out a call for young collegians to again help OMS reach a new generation of Japanese with the Gospel

Since this book is a composite of testimonies of various crusaders, I have used my initials, EE, when speaking of my own experiences.

There were 30 of us crusaders, mostly collegians or seminarians, who volunteered to join ECC. Nearly every one of us later stated that the 1950s to 60s crusade in Japan, Korea, Taiwan and Hong Kong forever changed our lives.

Ed Erny
2012
Greenwood, Indiana

Chapter 1

TRANSITION

With the conclusion of World War II came the birth of many new evangelical movements and organizations. OMS President Lettie Cowman, a saintly leader and a woman of vision and charisma, had reached her 80th birthday. Although still bright and alert, she was now finding it difficult to supply the necessities required by the demands of this period of great opportunity. At the time, OMS had just four fields in Asia and one in South America.

In faith missions of the type popularized by George Mueller and Hudson Taylor, missionaries were not responsible for raising their own support. All income and gifts were pooled and then divided among the missionaries. The result too often was that the few homeland personnel in leadership were left to bear the brunt of the financial concerns and confront the urgent demands of creditors. This they did through funding letters and soliciting support from local churches and Christian organizations. OMS' accounts were now perpetually in arrears. Missionaries for decades had received $100 a month, and even this minimal sum was seldom received on time. Each month that funds were not in hand, a letter went out to explain the financial straits, advising missionaries that in view of the deficits they should pray, trust God, and try to understand that their allowances would of necessity arrive a week or two late. Every six months or so, salaries were a full month behind and missionaries asked to forego an entire month's pay. This pattern usually meant only receiving 10 months' allowance for a 12-month period. These extremities also created havoc for the homeland office struggling to pay bills and often facing shortages of crisis' portions for items, not only for salaries but also for homeland workers, maintenance, postage, and printing. The kindly printer, Mr. Johnson, was again and again advised that he would be paid "in good time," which in simple terms meant later and later.

Eventually, this state of affairs was made known to the OMS board of trustees which, at this time, consisted entirely of President Lettie Cowman and OMS field leaders. To these were later added a few outstanding businessmen, Christian educators, ministers, and well-known evangelists.

With the advance in aviation occasioned by World War II, trans-Pacific flights were now possible. Hence, in 1949, OMS field leaders were advised to fly home to headquarters in Los Angeles, primarily for the purpose of electing a new president to take the place of Lettie Cowman. This decision had in no way been instigated or approved by President Lettie Cowman herself. As the men left their posts in Asia and South America, none fully imagined what lay ahead.

In the first board meetings that fall of 1949, Lettie proposed and more or less assumed her continuance as mission president. However, it soon became clear that the board, apprised of the mission's fiscal dilemma and their president's declining mental acuity, would in no way countenance their beloved leader's assumption. It was now inevitable that a change must be made.

The meetings dragged on from week to week. Lettie now put forth an alternate plan: that the board elect her protégé, Ben Pearson, a recent acquisition from the Free Methodist Church where he had ably headed up the entire denomination's youth department. Though the board held Ben Pearson in high esteem, he had been with OMS but a short time and had little in-depth knowledge of the mission. Another faction felt that, after Lettie's retirement and the long years of predominantly Cowman leadership, someone less under Cowman influence should be elected. Bud Kilbourne was the nominee. This would likely begin a Kilbourne era, with three outstanding sons, Ed, Elmer and Ernie, waiting in the wings.

This proposition had a number of supporters but not the required majority. Weeks followed with hours of prayer as well as sessions of heated debate. Eventually it became clear that the Kilbourne nomination would not gain a quorum. This left the board with but one choice and that was a dark-horse candidate who hopefully would be acceptable to some degree to the majority. After all, this was how Abraham Lincoln had been elected president in the fateful election of 1860.

Several now put forward the name of Eugene Erny. Although admittedly a capable executive and dynamic preacher, he was still in his 40s and viewed as a most important component in the advance of the mission in the fledgling India field. Long prayer meetings and discussions followed and, in the end, Eugene Erny was elected president of OMS.

CHAPTER 2

A NEW PRESIDENT

Though this choice was not entirely satisfactory to the entire board, the vote carried. Eugene and family were now required to leave India and locate at OMS headquarters in Los Angeles by January of 1950, when the inauguration ceremonies were set. Concurrent with Eugene's inauguration, there would be the celebration of Lettie's 80th birthday. This festive event to which all OMS personnel and supporters were invited was designated "Life Begins at 80."

In view of what Lettie considered an unwelcome turn of events, she announced that she would be resigning from OMS. A short time later she revealed that she intended to establish two new organizations. The first would promote and sell her books and was named Cowman Publications. The other organization would concern itself primarily with promoting and carrying on Charles' vision of Gospel distribution to every home and would be known as Gospel Crusades. Lettie also made it clear that since OMS had "turned her out" she would take with her the property rights to her very famous and lucrative books, particularly *Streams in the Desert*.

This news came as a most painful shock to the mission's leadership and new president. In financial extremities which seemed to threaten its very survival, OMS would now be bereft of its single greatest source of income, the sales of *Streams in the Desert*. This happened despite the fact that Lettie's books from the start had all been registered under the OMS name and hence were legally OMS property. In Lettie's mind the books were entirely her property with freedom to do with them as she pleased.

Eugene, as a young man of high school age, had been made vice-president of the Erny family lumber and manufacturing business with offices in Chicago. The company was a major supplier of containers for Kraft Food products and other large companies, such as the great Marshall Field's Department Store. Since his father was a semi-invalid due to a crippling bout of encephalitis, the burden of the management fell on Eugene's youthful shoulders. Lettie Cowman later said approvingly of Eugene, "My husband Charles was also a businessman. It takes considerable executive and managerial gifts to run a mission. How wonderful our new president has a background of experience in business."

Eugene had also been blessed with the gift of public speaking and eloquence of the Paul Rader and Henry Clay Morrison variety. As a youth Eugene had attended Paul Rader's famous Moody Tabernacle in Chicago. An heroic all-American athlete, Rader preached with fervor and volume, riveting the hearer's attention. Eugene's covenant and passion, struck at the altar of Austin Tabernacle in Chicago under the anointing of the Holy Spirit, came forth like hot lava from a fire-spewing volcano.

In coming to office, Eugene quickly became cognizant of both OMS' paucity of missionaries and alarmingly depleted treasury. Within a year he had convinced the board to adopt the increasingly popular self-funding policy. Thus each missionary, including executives, office workers, and even maintenance people would depend on God to supply their need. They were to exert every effort to raise their own allowance, amounting to the designated MSR or Missionary Share Requirement set by the mission.

Now every missionary was required to recruit a personal "support team"—family, friends, and churches—that promised to help provide regular support, altogether totaling about $100 a month. This was a daunting prospect for OMS personnel with little or no experience in fundraising. For them, a bold exercise of faith was required. The blessed practical result and benefit of this system meant that now a few homeland executives did not have to bear almost the full burden of funding the entire mission, including the personal support of every missionary.

Under the new plan, an OMS missionary could leave for the field only after he had raised his full support for a term of five years. With post-World War II inflation, the cost of supporting a missionary increased and the monthly share quota was raised accordingly. How God faithfully supplied the ever-increasing share needs each term with totals soaring to 30, 40, 50, 100 or 200 $5-shares makes a lively narrative. Even missionaries with the most trepidation saw their needs met. And with the increasing number of required shares came a commensurate increase in friends and shareholders, as well as prayer support. Today many missionary families have a support team numbering several hundred persons who have at some time and to some degree supported them. To sustain their supporters' interest, missionaries keep in regular contact with reports providing personal prayer requests and accounts of God's provisions and blessings.

Once this plan was instituted, OMS' financial crises were virtually eliminated and the entire mission was put on a sound financial footing. More than this, the new financial plan resulted in a large flock of new candidates, rapidly increasing the size of OMS, a mission which for half a century never had more than 40 or 50 missionaries.

Chapter 3

THE VISION LIVES

As a young missionary, Eugene had participated in The Great Village Campaign (later renamed the Every Creature Crusade) in China and India. He knew, too, that the crusades were responsible for attracting some of the mission's finest personnel, men like Harry Woods, John Miller, and Paul Haines. They had helped to establish OMS work in Japan and Korea. Harry Woods had evangelized Okinawa before joining the pioneers in China where he soon became field director.

Eugene Erny had been recruited for OMS as a result of the Asbury College Missionary Team tour in 1929-30. His teammates, Byron Crouse and Virgil Kirkpatrick, would forever after be undying friends and supporters of missions, Kirkpatrick himself a missionary to Africa. On this tour Eugene had observed the effectiveness of The Great Village Campaign in Japan and Korea. Why not, then, a vigorous program to recruit another team of American crusaders from the post-World War II generation? They would once more target every home in Japan and other Asian countries. The timeliness of this decision was affirmed when General Douglas MacArthur called for thousands of missionaries to go to Japan. Shouldn't OMS be part of that?

Eugene was elected president of The Oriental Missionary Society in the fall of 1949, the same year his son Robert graduated from Woodstock, the famed India missionary school in the foothills of the Himalayas. When early in 1950 the Ernys had flown to Los Angeles, the memorable trip required flying over the so-called "hump" of the Himalayas, the highest mountains in the world. Approaching Hong Kong, where the airport runway at that time

7

was little more than a narrow ledge hewn out of the surrounding hills, they encountered bad weather. Heavy clouds lay like a dark ceiling above the narrow runway. The atmosphere at this time produced numerous air pockets. As the plane circled the airport, it had to negotiate these treacherous vacuums which sent their Pan-Am plane hurling as it were straight down an elevator-shaft. The pilot aided by much prayer summoned all his skill to effect a safe and perfect landing, but Eugene's wife, Esther, forever after shunned air travel.

In Hong Kong the Ernys boarded a troop carrier, the Marine Gordon, for the voyage to the U.S. On the fearfully over-crowded ship were a great many refugees fleeing Communist China. Women and children were given semi-private staterooms. Men-folk, however, had no such luxury and slept in two-tiered bunk beds, military style.

As Dad settled into the L.A. office, he took stock of the small mission. Though greatly used of God, OMS was little known outside holiness circles in Eastern and mid-Western states. There had been almost no increase in personnel in 50 years. The total income for 1950 was about $500,000, a pitifully small sum for an entire mission, even in those days.

OMS had always operated on a strictly egalitarian basis. All missionaries were paid the same with a janitor receiving a salary equal to that of the president. I recall my years in high school, when from my meager savings, I helped Dad buy the then-requisite seat covers for the mission car. Of course, in our home there was no money for a coveted television set during this feverish inauguration of the TV era. My junior year of high school I put together from my earnings $75 (money I'd received from painting OMS houses) and bought the family TV. Many of

8

the personnel at headquarters lived in single rooms and shared a kitchen with the other office staff. This inconvenience, however, did a great deal to create the famed OMS "family spirit."

Once settled into his office, Eugene reviewed factors that in the past had contributed to the mission's growth and attracted a number of her finest missionaries. The mission held, without apology, the view that Christ's great commission to go into all the world was to be taken quite literally. It was this that had propelled the mission and her Japan Holiness Church to its pre-war status as the nation's third largest denomination. It had also contributed to the explosive growth of the Korean Holiness Church. Almost all OMS missionaries of that era had been involved in these Every Creature Crusades. Among them were Harry Woods, Rolland Rice, Uri Chandler, Rosalind Rinker, and Eugene himself. So it was that shortly after Eugene took office he announced the launching of a second crusade beginning again in Japan.

In 1950, articles began to appear in the OMS magazine, *The Missionary Standard*, announcing that in response to MacArthur's call for missionaries but even more in response to Christ's command to go into all the world, OMS would again recruit young men to place the Word of God in every home in Japan. The mission magazine, then issued every month, carried on its back cover a large conspicuous call for young men to give two and a half years and join national teams to evangelize Japan. Those who had already enlisted were boldly pictured. Underneath were words in large type: **CALLING FOR TEN YOUNG MEN FOR CRUSADES TO JAPAN.** Then in smaller letters: Single men, Bible college or college graduates desired. Write for information at once.

The magazine, at this time, being mailed out to about 20,000 homes, was perhaps the means by which most participants first learned of the crusade. In addition, however, there was never a time when the mission had so many effective recruiters. In the wake of World War II, a good many younger men, who had been exposed to the heart-wrenching needs of the nations, were now sensing a missionary call, particularly to Asia. Added to this was the impact of a fresh wave of revivals, as well as the Billy Graham crusades challenging youth to take their cross and follow Christ. The slogan of one mission was "Come, Live, Die."

Chapter 4

RECRUITING YOUNG MEN

At no other time had OMS possessed so many firebrands, bold men whose messages were a strong summons, calling youth to heroics and hardships for Jesus. Eugene, as a collegian, had organized a dynamic team that spent their summers holding tent revivals all over the central and eastern U.S. Upon graduation he and his fellow evangelists set out on an evangelistic tour throughout Asia and the Middle East. They were gone an entire year. Here again emerged the spirit of A.B. Simpson, so bent on fulfilling Christ's great commission that he named his new association of churches The Christian and Missionary Alliance. It was he who had so powerfully influenced Charles and Lettie to be missionaries, thus helping to birth The Oriental Missionary Society.

Among OMS' most effective communicators and recruiters was Charles Putts Culver, formerly both a diplomat and missionary in China. He was considered by many to be OMS' most powerful orator. William Gillam, also an excellent speaker, gifted musician, and a man of unusual fervency, represented the mission on many campuses. Dale McClain, a missionary to China, India and Hong Kong, was also a dynamic speaker. He traveled widely to colleges, Bible schools and churches. A born huckster and salesman by nature who could have filled the big top anywhere, he now invested his gift of the "sound and fury" for the sake of Jesus. Others who helped spread the Every Creature Crusade vision included Paul Haines, Jr. and Roy Adams.

Added to these were the dynamic Kilbourne brothers, Ed, Elmer and Ernie, all of whom had to a greater or lesser degree inherited their mother Hazel's magnetic personality and oratorical gifts. Some called Hazel the best woman speaker they had ever heard.

As this contingent of empowered missionaries was sent on recruitment tours, their first targets were evangelical colleges, primarily those of Wesleyan persuasion, both in the U.S. and Canada. The first and most productive school was Asbury College. Asbury had important historic ties with OMS, thanks in part to the missionary trio headed by Eugene Erny who toured the world in 1929-30.

During the 1950s, the Asbury campus had twice been visited by revivals that rank among some of the most powerful and influential in the nation's history. The first in recent times erupted in 1950, a second in 1958, and then a third in 1970. These revivals all broke out on the campus after prolonged periods of prayer. In the wake of these revivals, Asbury teams traveled throughout the U.S., and the fire spread to scores of churches and Christian colleges. Chief recruiting grounds, along with Asbury College, were Azusa College in California; Taylor University in Upland, Indiana; Ft. Wayne Bible College; Hesston College in Kansas; and Cascade College and Western Evangelical Seminary in Oregon. In Canada, where OMS enlisted some of her finest candidates, Hillcrest College was a most fruitful recruiting ground.

Strange to say, the once-intimate ties that existed between God's Bible School and OMS had now greatly weakened, this despite the fact that the original American participants for The Great Village Campaign had all been GBS men. Several factors account for this. About 1916, the National Holiness Association, a large group of churches loyal to the views of John Wesley and the Methodist Church, decided to organize their own mission society which would be named the National Holiness Missionary Society (NHMS). They had first appealed to Cowman and Kilbourne to designate OMS as the official holiness mission, but neither Cowman nor Kilbourne felt led to accept this generous offer. Thus another mission was organized under the NHMS name. This name was later changed to World Gospel Mission (WGM). It should also be mentioned that for an interval God's Bible School and the Wesleyan Church both designated OMS as their approved mission organization. The Wesleyan Church later organized its own mission.

In time, Asbury College relinquished some of its more conservative standards relative to matters of dress and jewelry while GBS retained them. Though the mission to this day has a deep appreciation for GBS, by the mid-1940s, most of OMS missionaries had ties to Asbury College (now Asbury University) and Asbury Theological Seminary.

Instead of serving a term of one year, this new generation of crusaders would be required to give a full two and a half years. This change particularly impacted the six young men, who at the time of their call, were engaged to be married. It would mean postponing their weddings for a period of time which for most of them seemed a small eternity.

Not only would the term of service be twice as long as the first crusade, this time there was no wealthy patron available to bear the young men's living and travel costs as was the case in 1917. The second generation of crusaders would be required to raise their own support to the amount of $100 per month, the equivalent of a full OMS missionary salary.

The prospect of raising their own support was for most of the aspiring candidates quite intimidating. A few came from large, mission-minded churches and garnered the entire requisite amount in a single Sunday. Others came from wealthy families that assured their sons "whatever deficit you have we'll make up. I don't want my child going around asking for money." Most, however, came from small churches and possessed no great family wealth. This calling meant trusting God all the way, pure and simple.

Having grown up in a faith mission, I (EE) had been taught that giving others opportunity to send a missionary to unreached peoples was truly tantamount to helping them lay up treasures in heaven, treasures worth more than the world, for which they would "someday thank you." Still I was assaulted by doubts and fears. As I drove to my first missionary meeting, a small country church in Virginia pastored by friendly Asburians, I was full of trepidation. By the end of the weekend to my amazement and joyous surprise, several persons had promised to support me at $5 a month for my entire term on the field. More amazing the pastor and his wife took a share in me and continued to support us for nearly 50 years.

Chapter 5

THE INEXORABLE CALL

In 1952, one of the first to respond to the OMS crusade call was Frances (Frank) Davis. Frank was born in Akron, Ohio, in 1920. After high school he landed a job as a lab assistant, studying evenings in Polytechnic Institute of Brooklyn. During the early 40s, he worked in a war plant. Then in 1943 Frank was drafted into the Air Force and sent to the South Pacific. The testimony of a fellow GI put Frank under conviction. "Out there, under the wing of a B26," he recalls, "I read a tract sent out by Marion College, Indiana (now Indiana Wesleyan University), and I received Christ as my Savior." Later when stationed in Tokyo, Frank served as a chaplain's assistant. After the war he enrolled in Houghton College in New York and upon graduation entered Asbury Seminary. "One term," Frank says, "Eugene Erny challenged us to go to Japan as evangelistic crusaders for two years."

Another of the earliest crusaders was Charles Dupree. At Asbury College he met and became engaged to JoAnn McClure. "Both of us felt called as missionaries to South America," he says, "but one day in chapel Bill Gillam, then on furlough from South America, spoke about the newly-instituted Every Creature Crusade in Japan." After the service Chuck spoke with Bill seeking counsel about applying to OMS for Latin America. Curiously Bill, himself a missionary to Colombia, had only Japan and MacArthur's urgent call for missionaries on his mind. After prayer Chuck agreed to postpone their wedding and South America plans until he had finished a two and a half year crusade term in Japan. Chuck and JoAnn never did get to South America as missionaries. Upon graduation from Asbury Seminary, they

15

sailed for Tokyo and the campus of Tokyo Bible Seminary. Later, Chuck was mightily used of God in planning and building the OMS summer camp on Oshima Island in the Tokyo Bay. This ministry has been instrumental in the salvation of hundreds of Japanese youth, many of whom enrolled in OMS' Tokyo Bible Seminary.

Another one of the early crusaders was Lowell Williamson. Lowell was the only crusader whose father had taken part in the initial Great Village Campaign of 1917. When Everett Williamson learned that a second crusade was being planned, he urged his son, Lowell, to go to Winona Lake where the OMS international convention was being held. Moved by the OMS vision to once again take God's Word to every home in Japan, Lowell signed up for the program. Later he was chosen to transfer to Taiwan and help initiate the Every Creature Crusade in that country.

Lowell joined the second crusade in 1952 following two years of schooling, first at Findlay College in Ohio and a year at Asbury College. Unlike most of the other crusaders, Lowell while a student had pastored a church and had considerable experience preaching.

Helmut Schultz was the son of German immigrants from Russia who had fled to Canada after World War I and the devastation of the Communist revolution. Saved in a church on the prairies of Alberta, he ended up at Hillcrest College.

Missionaries occasionally visited Hillcrest and from them Helmut first heard of The Oriental Missionary Society. About that time a friend sent him the OMS magazine, *The Standard*. On the back cover in bold letters was a plea for 21 young men to join the new

Every Creature Crusade. The magazine told of the first crusade called The Great Village Campaign carried out under Cowman and Kilbourne's leadership. Now in the post-World War II years, OMS was launching the second crusade. Helmut sensed God calling him to join this venture but the thought of himself becoming a foreign missionary seemed quite incredible. In order to "prove" his call, he devised a Gideon-like scheme to hopefully confirm his calling—or better yet excuse him from a task for which he imagined himself totally unworthy.

Wesley Wildermuth, OMS missionary in Japan and later field leader, remembers the day the field committee reviewed the application from the young Canadian: "As the committee looked it over, we had some serious reservations about the boy's qualifications. The form was filled out in pencil, barely legible. Answers were vague. In response to the question, 'What experience have you had in Christian work?' he had simply written, 'I once taught a Sunday School class.'" Upon the advice of their field leader, Dr. Roy Adams, the committee all voted to reject the application of Helmut Schultz.

For some reason, never fully explained, OMS headquarters did something unusual and possibly unprecedented. They overruled the decision of the Japan field committee and accepted the young candidate. OMS then advised the field that Helmut Schultz would be arriving in Japan in a few months to join the crusade.

"When we received this information," Wes Wildermuth recalled, "we were not pleased. Why did OMS even send us the application if they refused to honor our decision?"

The day came when the Japan missionaries went to the wharf to meet Helmut Schultz. "Down the gangplank he came,"

Wildermuth remembers, "a gangly, self-conscious blond young man who spoke with a slight German-Canadian accent. Could this youth actually be missionary material?"

"All of our questions," says Art Shelton, "were laid to rest at that first weekly prayer meeting. When we heard Helmut pray, his fervent passion clearly indicated a wonderful familiarity with his Lord." "In an instant," adds Wesley, "all of our doubts dissolved. And, then as we sat listening to his testimony, we were amazed at his spiritual depth." Helmut was destined to one day be the OMS Japan field leader and later the mission's vice-president.

The story of how I (EE) came to enlist in this second crusade in 1958 remains in my mind as a drama second in importance only to my salvation. When the Every Creature Crusade program was presented to me in 1958, it was just prior to the outbreak of a great Asbury College revival. This event set in motion tremendous turmoil within my spirit. The problem now was that I had no intention of leaving the U.S. immediately. What totally dominated my thoughts during those days was my pending wedding to Rachel. I reasoned that after we were married and my seminary education completed, the next step would be foreign missions, probably India where I had grown up. Those were the wonderful and sensible plans in my mind, the whole matter completely logical and firmly resolved. Then, the worst thing possible happened—I got a call!

The 1958 revival broke upon the campus of Asbury College with torrential power one morning in March, my first year in Asbury Theological Seminary located across Lexington Avenue from the college. It started spontaneously in a routinely scheduled chapel and continued day and night without intermission. Delegations from churches all over America began to arrive in Wilmore to discover what God was doing on the campus.

Rachel and I were deeply in love and our wedding date set for the first of June, only a few weeks away. As I sat in Hughes Auditorium, there came a growing and terrible certainty that my departure for Asia was to be immediate and must in no way be postponed to a future date after we were married. As clearly as if I had heard audible words, the inner voice asked, "Are you willing to postpone your wedding for two and a half years and go overseas as a crusader?" My initial response was, "I will put these foolish notions out of my mind. The issue is settled. I will soon be married and upon completion of my seminary degree, we will indeed be foreign missionaries."

But as the saying goes, "Man proposes, God disposes." Strange and terrible thoughts began coursing through my mind. What if I were to disobey the Lord? I would certainly miss His highest calling for my life. Day after day I found it impossible to sleep nor could I study. It became a torment to attend the ongoing revival meetings. Words of scripture kept floating through my mind. I Samuel 15: 22, "Obedience is greater than sacrifice;" Acts 26:14, "Saul, Saul, it is hard for you to kick against the goad;" and especially John 21:15 and Jesus' words to Peter, "Peter, Peter, lovest thou me more than these?" Scholars debate the meaning of the word "these." Did "these" mean the nets that had drawn Peter back to fishing? Or possibly the word "these" referred to the other disciples? But as far as I was concerned, without question, "these" represented our wedding plans. The long days of torment and my final capitulation to the will of God marked a kind of spiritual crisis for me that changed my life in ways far beyond my comprehension at that time. I often reflect on how different my life would have been without that crisis of obedience. Oswald

Chamber once said to his students: "God cannot do much with a man until He hurts him." Hard words, but true.

Chapter 6

ORIENTATION

In Japan Rolland Rice, a former China missionary, was directing the crusade. He and his wife, Mildred, were destined to become something of a legend in OMS. Rollie was the son of E.O. Rice who had at one time been a well-known banker, a friend of Henry Ford, and later served as the treasurer of Taylor University. At an advanced age, he moved to Los Angeles and assisted OMS in the Mail Department.

Rolland was a veteran of The Great Village Campaign in China. When forced to leave China, he and his family moved to Japan. From the start the crusade under Rolland's leadership utilized army surplus tents which were readily available from the U.S. military still stationed in Japan. The largest area of the tent was occupied by anywhere from 50 to 100 chairs. In the back part, a small area (in some tents no larger than six by seven feet) was the living quarters. The crusaders slept either on air mattresses or grass mats called tatamis. The Japanese team leader would engage a local woman to cook for them. She prepared meals over a small charcoal burner and, during the day when the team was away in distribution, she also served as watchman making sure that none of our goods were pilfered or any other mischief occurred.

When Lowell Williamson arrived in Japan, Rolland met him. Lowell recalls:

Rollie simply drove me around Tokyo to introduce me to my new home. At that time, OMS had not yet developed any program of orientation nor did they give us fledgling missionaries any language study.

On my third day in Japan, Rollie gave me the keys to the crusade van. I learned that I was to also serve as chauffer for our team. He took me to the site where the crusade was already in progress and introduced me to my Japanese teammates. I grabbed my sleeping bag and clothes and joined the men in the back of the tent. There I was with not a word of Japanese other than "sukiyaki," no orientation, and no written job description. I sometimes wonder how I survived.

Rolland had many gifts, not the least of which was music. He played the violin beautifully and with his wife sang duets. Rolland had been one of the early missionaries in China in the 1930s working with Eugene Erny and Uri Chandler in The Great Village Campaign of North China. The Rice's tenure in China, however, was twice cut short, first by the invasion of Japanese in 1937 and again in 1949 when Communist armies under Mao Tse Tung completed their conquest of the China mainland and the expulsion of most foreign missionaries.

Rolland was a man of great zeal and a wonderful sense of humor. He learned Chinese well and had no qualms about witnessing to virtually everyone he met whether on the street or in a train. He designed small pins displaying a heart out of which rose a scarlet flame of fire. These he gave to all the missionaries and crusaders, explaining that they represented "The Fellowship of the Flaming Heart" of which they were now members.

When I (EE) joined the second crusade, arriving in Taiwan in September 1958, I found that Rolland was the field leader. What great times we had and we both loved tennis. Like many gifted men, however, Rolland was hopelessly absentminded. He once traveled to Japan and distractedly threw his return air ticket in the waste basket. On another occasion he went to the huge downtown railway station, bought his ticket, and walked away without his briefcase.

During my first stint in the Taiwan crusade, we scheduled a meeting for Rollie. He was to preach, play his violin, and also show a film. Though Rollie spoke Mandarin fluently, he was not familiar with the local Taiwanese dialect used in rural areas. He assured me he would bring an interpreter with him. En route to our crusade site, he suddenly remembered that he had forgotten his violin. He rushed back, retrieved the violin, and arrived at the service a half hour late. We were concerned, however, since he had come without an interpreter. "Rollie," we asked, "where is your interpreter?" He paused a moment, clapped his hand to his head and sighed, "Oh, my! I left him sitting on the front porch!"

Everyone who knew Rollie well had some anecdote of this sort. The Rices were not only deeply spiritual and zealous leaders but also cherished friends. Rollie died of a heart attack at age 60 but Mildred, an OMS legend and subject of the book, *The Key Goose*, lived another 30 years. During this time we had the precious opportunity of constant correspondence with her and many delightful visits at her home in Los Angeles.

As our crusade continued, the OMS' early, impromptu welcome for new arrivals gave way to a proper orientation. After a week or so, it was time to leave the gracious environs of the OMS campus. Crusaders were now scheduled to join their teams at one of the sites where meetings were usually in progress. The routine was to stay out in the field during the week but return to the compound for some R and R each weekend. This was a blessed provision, especially in the early months when all of the crusaders were experiencing, often for the first time in their lives, severe homesickness and culture shock.

In Japan the OMS field director at this time was Roy Adams. After his first wife died, he had married Elizabeth, a sweet, good-natured lady, who endeared herself to all of us crusaders. Helmut Schultz remembers Roy as "the best Bible expositor I ever heard. He had a tremendous influence upon the lives of the young crusaders and I will forever be in his debt."

When several crusaders arrived on the field at about the same time, Roy would schedule a special retreat for them, providing information on Japan and all that awaited them and also kindling in their hearts the message and fire of the Holy Spirit.

Chapter 7

LOST IN TOKYO

One crusader whose introduction to Japan was probably the most memorable was Dick Amos, an Asburian from Texas, who was then engaged to Judy Gillam, daughter of Colombian Field Director Bill Gillam. He remembers:

The day after I arrived in Japan in November 1958, two other short-termers and I were on our way to the nearby missionary children's school to play basketball. We left the OMS compound by the back gate and wound our way to the station via small back alleys. I was completely disoriented after the second turn, but I knew the guys were familiar with the route so I had no fear.

We bought our tickets at the Okubo station and rode to the next stop to change lines. As we started to board the train, the other guys jumped aboard, but I courteously let everyone enter ahead of me. Just as I started to get on the train, the doors suddenly shut in my face. The guys merrily waved goodbye as the train pulled out. I was not too concerned and felt sure that my friends would wait for me at the next station. I calmly caught the next train, expecting in a few minutes to see their smiling faces. They, however, thought I would wait for them where we last parted. So while they returned to our original station, I rode the train from one stop to another, earnestly and increasingly anxious, hoping for a glimpse of my friends.

I rode for about one hour scanning the crowds at every station. I did not know that the train line made a circle around the entire city of Tokyo. I must have been almost back to the original station when I decided to get off the train and return in the direction from which I had come. Having just arrived in Japan, I didn't know the name of any station so I rode for another hour. I realized I had left the compound without either the telephone number or address of OMS. I now decided to go out in front of a station and seek out a helpful friend who could speak English. For the first time in my life, I was truly a stranger in a strange land. Desperately I looked for help. I asked many people if they could assist me and always got the same answer in perfect English, "I don't speak English." That was the limit of their knowledge of my language and before the day was over I had decided some day I must teach English in Japan.

The only Japanese I knew at that time were two phrases: the morning greeting, "ohio gozimas, and "peko-peko," I'm hungry. After standing in front of Shinjuku Station for six hours, it was now afternoon and my first Japanese phrase was useless. But I was really feeling "peko-peko" since I had not eaten lunch and it was approaching supper time. I had left the compound with 180 yen, and I had used half of that on a futile attempt to call OMS using a wrong number that a policeman had given me. So with a meager 90 yen in my pocket, I just stood in front of a camera store across from Shinjuku Station, waiting to be rescued. What I did not know was that our very worried missionaries were conducting a vain search for me, a quest that took them all over the city and finally to the Tokyo city morgue. Gratefully, they did not find my remains there on a slab.

Finally, a Japanese man with somewhat more English then the others came up to me and asked what I was doing. He was, in fact, the owner of the camera store where I had been standing for eight hours. He had noticed me when he closed shop at five o'clock and now four hours later, returning from supper, questioned why I was still standing there.

That kind gentleman was indeed the answer to my increasingly urgent prayers. He knew of the OMS-related Bible school so drew an excellent map. I showed it to a taxi driver, motioned frantically, and said, "Go! Go! Go!" The five-minute ride to the school cost 70 yen so I had 20 yen left in my pocket when I arrived back at the Bible School campus. I've never been more warmly welcomed. Along with energetic hugs, there were "Hallelujahs" and "Praise the Lords." Our director's wife, Aunt Lizzie Adams, a generously proportioned lady, approached me with an embrace I'll never forget.

Lloyd Fitch (R), interpreter, Rolland Rice, crusade director – 1952

Lowell Williamson and interpreter

Japanese crusaders (R to L); Messers. Kimura, Nihira, Mori, Kikuchi, Watanabe

1952 Crusader Frank Davis, wife Martha and children

Worshipping ancestors at Japanese funeral – circa 1955

Threshing grain

Terraced rice fields

Japanese farmer

Plowing

Maids in spring

Austin Boggan, 1953

Hudson Hess, 1957

Crusade meeting

*Austin Boggan with
Korean orphans*

New believer burning idols

Missionary Standard ad- 1954

GOAL

The goal of this Crusade is to reach every home as far as possible in the entire nation of Japan with the Gospel. During the past year four Crusade teams composed of a missionary leader with six Japanese were engaged in this task, but we aim to send out twenty-five teams as soon as possible.

OBJECTIVES OF THE CRUSADE

- The free distribution of Gospel portions, explanatory and Gospel tracts to every home in Japan.

- The effective preaching of the Gospel through personal witnessing and public meetings with the prayerful and earnest expectation that men and women, young and old, will seek and find Christ as Savior.

- The establishing of all new believers into indigenous churches under the supervision of Japanese leaders.

$10 WILL COVER THE COST OF EVANGELISM IN ONE VILLAGE.

ACCOMPLISHMENTS OF THE CRUSADE

- Covering a period of 22 months approximately 500,000 Gospels and tracts respectively have been distributed to the same number of homes by the Crusade Teams.

- Approximately 17,000 men and women, boys and girls have sought the Lord during the same period of time.

- Thirty-three new groups of believers have been organized during this period and are meeting in regular worship services. Twenty-eight groups have also been added to already established churches.

$50 WILL COVER THE APPROXIMATE COST OF ONE TENT CAMPAIGN.

| Rolland Rice | Francis Davis | Charles Dupree | Dale Neff | Bob Holland | Lloyd Fitch | Lowell Williamson | Charles Kempin |

Chapter 8

DOGS AND OTHER DANGERS

Chuck Dupree remembers that one of the most aggravating aspects of house-to-house distribution lay in the fact that almost every rural Japanese home was guarded by one or more dogs.

Most of them were of a small red breed. They were likely not very vicious but they were all champion barkers, and it was impossible to tell which one of them might be bold enough to actually attack us. Gratefully we carried our literature in shoulder bags, and these proved to be excellent defensive weapons against these canines which would frequently lunge at us. Many of the dogs were chained, and we were careful to measure the length of their restraints. In one instance, however, upon entering a courtyard, I discovered that the tether on this vicious animal had somehow broken. I could see that he was quite determined to take a large bite of flesh out of my thigh. Fortunately, there was a tree nearby and, though I had never been a champion tree climber, this time I surprised myself by gaining a perch on one of the upper limbs in no time flat. In the process though, I had dropped my literature bag and now our precious tracts and booklets were scattered all over the yard. I sat there for a while contemplating what my next move should be. I glanced over toward the nearby rice field and to my dismay found that a young lady, likely the proprietor of this small home, was watching my plight, and the tree climbing drama was clearly affording her great delight. In time she came to my rescue, chained the dog, and helped me gather my literature. With some muttered words of gratitude, I proceeded to the next house.

All of the crusaders have a fund of anecdotes involving "haifu" or door-to-door Gospel distribution Some of our early faux pas were truly hilarious.

Another Asburian from Aden, North Carolina, was Kemp Edwards. He and I (EE) had traveled together in deputation and then been cabin mates in 1958 when together we voyaged across the Pacific on a Danish ship, the Laura Maersk. He tells of a particularly embarrassing moment:

One afternoon my Japanese partner and I were delivering Gospel booklets to homes. We were out in a remote village area. I approached a farmhouse entrance and as usual, instead of knocking on the door or anything so crude, it was customary to softly call out "gomen kudasai" which means "I'm here." The large paper door opened and a beautiful Japanese girl with a baby on her back appeared. I bowed, she bowed. I bowed, she bowed. Finally I managed to utter the words that I had been taught to say when handing someone "The Way of Life" booklet. The phrase was "Please take this book and read it," which translated into Japanese is "dozo o yomi ni natte kudasai." As I spoke these carefully-rehearsed words, suddenly the girl's eyes widened. She looked startled. Then she grabbed the booklet and raced back up the steps and into the house. This was not the response I had been hoping for. At that point my young Japanese partner smilingly asked, "Sensei, do you know what you said?" I looked at him doubtfully and replied, "I think I do. I told her to please take the book and read it." Here my teammate, stifling a laugh, said,

"Well, no, that's not exactly what you said. Instead of saying "dozo o yomi," which means "please read," you said "o youmi ni natte," which means "will you please marry me?"!

Stanley Dyer from Canada, who with his wife, Joanna, devoted more than over 40 years to missions in Japan and then served as the OMS Canada director, remembers that one of the most difficult aspects of the crusade was what he called a humbling experience of failure. He recalls:

> I came to realize that a young man's dreams of great, earth-shaking ministry may not immediately come to fruition. One of our tent campaigns was held in the large city of Kobe, a very densely populated area. I felt sure that we would see great numbers attending our services and coming to Christ. I thought to myself, "This will make a fine story for my next prayer letter, maybe even a feature in the next issue of the OMS magazine, *The Standard.*"

> Things did not turn out quite as I had imagined. At the end of the campaign, we could count only one who had been saved. I was encouraged, however, that he seemed a very promising young man. He actually began working with us in Gospel distribution.

> One day we assigned him to guard the tent and our belongings while we went out for hours of house-to-house "haifu." When we returned, our prize convert was no where in sight. We looked about and noticed that not only was he gone but also absent was my accordion, radio, blankets, clothing, and money. Only one convert, I

thought to myself, and he turned out to be a Judas. What a failure I was. What an unworthy and utter failure!

I spent an entire night in prayer, wrestling with God. He humbled me and made me realize that all ministry belongs to Him and comes from Him. This was truly an experience that changed my life. As for the malefactor who had so cruelly betrayed us, he was apprehended. I had taken a photograph of the young man for posterity—the shining convert of that difficult campaign! I had the film developed and delivered a copy of that photo to the police who in short order caught and jailed the man.

Chapter 9

NOT THE RITZ

Winters in Japan can be fearfully cold and often, when it became too frigid to live in the unheated tents, the team would move for a time into a rented room. For one team it was a loft above a garage.

Lowell Williamson describes his early days in Japan:

Adjusting to the spartan living conditions of the itinerant evangelist in a foreign land was one of the challenges. It was December when I joined the crusade and often snow was on the ground. We had no heat in the tent and nights turned bitter cold. Gratefully, it was later decided that during the winter months our teams should move from tents into rented rooms which were far warmer. Yet my sleeping bag was totally inadequate for the damp penetrating cold. I usually awakened several times at night—freezing! One morning, however, I awoke and discovered I was amazingly warm. Then I realized that during the night one of my teammates had spread his futon (quilt) over me. Since he now was too cold to sleep, he had spent the entire night praying. That's what I call enduring hardship for the sake of the Gospel. What brotherly love from these colleagues was poured out upon us.

Later, when the crusade was begun in Taiwan, the most densely-populated nation in the entire world, there was usually no room to pitch a tent within the city limits. Here, customarily, a large room serving as a Gospel hall was rented on the street level with sleeping accommodations above.

During those post-World War II years in Taiwan, when the average income was about fifty cents a day, I and my teammates had to put up with some truly miserable conditions. Adjacent to the "bedroom" where my air mattress was located was usually the latrine, the contents of which were not regularly emptied. In Tou Liu, the restroom was a mere hole in the ground where congregated large populations of maggots. The local English word for toilet in Taiwan was WC (water closet) as it is in much of the world. My Taiwanese teammates had a great sense of humor and one, gifted with artistic skill, inscribed an elaborate sign which read "WC—The Washington Club." This he nailed to the outhouse door. The boys insisted that we must have a picture taken, seated sedately in front of The Washington Club.

The worst feature of our quarters in Tou Liu was that the dwelling reposed above a local sewer, and through the generous cracks in the floorboard we could see large rats shuttling back and forth all day. Fortunately, mosquito nets were available, a truly blessed provision, which prevented not only mosquitoes from biting but also rats from galloping across our bodies. The crude kitchen was equipped with a charcoal stove and uncovered food made a perfect haven for cockroaches. Only a few of the creatures appeared during the day but at night it was high carnival. One night, needing a glass of water, I extricated myself from the mosquito net and made my way to the kitchen. When I turned on the light, it was as though the entire room was set in motion. What was this sudden frenzied movement? As I came to life and my eyes focused, I perceived there were a hundred or more (I counted them) hungry cockroaches in earnest quest of their evening repast.

Chapter 10

HE SPREADS A TABLE BEFORE ME

Perhaps the greatest trial for all of us was our seriously offended western palates and the relentless diet of rice, rice, and more rice accompanied by barely edible and strange vegetables, some of which we had never seen before.

The foreign crusaders ate the very same fare as their national colleagues. All of them lived at this time at a near poverty level, each putting his small share of yen or N.T. dollars in the common pot, enough to provide simple meals for the current month. In Taiwan, in 1959, the average income of our coworkers was $10 a month. Half of that ($5) paid for meals. The diet consisted primarily of coarse rice, cabbage and squash, along with small bits of fish and pork fat. For the nationals this was pretty much customary fare; for us wai-gwos (foreigners) the sound of the dinner bell often induced a kind of depression. Most of us crusaders, during the two-year stint, lost from 10 to 30 pounds. One profitable effect, however, was that living on this near-starvation diet for the first time in our lives, the absence of any desire for food made prolonged periods of fasting and prayer not only possible but desirable.

For Kelly Toth, his crusade was very nearly cut prematurely short by a most improbable allergy. He remembers:

When our team went to Fukushima, problems developed. I had been on a steady diet of rice, a grain I had seldom eaten. After some weeks this regimen started to take its toll on my health. Before long I had developed a full-blown allergy to rice. Pink spots began to emerge all over my body gradually becoming scarlet welts. These then grew larger and larger. At the same time I was also assaulted with a severe case of dysentery, which left me seriously dehydrated.

The public bathroom we used was half a block away and soon, the local policeman, seeing me hastening for relief, would immediately stop traffic to expedite my emergency flight. My weight dropped from 150 pounds to 115 in a little over a month. With no medical treatment, I lapsed into a near coma. The mission decided they would have to send me back home to Canada. However, my dear team members and our OMS missionaries prayed fervently for my healing. Miraculously, I began to improve and soon found myself able to eat rice without any adverse results. I learned, however, to limit the huge bowls of rice that the Japanese love. Praise God. My healing was to me a true miracle.

Kelly Toth speaks of another unusual encounter, not with a Japanese but with a fellow countryman:

One day I happened to be walking through town passing out tracts when a young American dressed in an Air Force uniform stopped me on the street and asked if I was in the military. During the American occupation of Japan, following the war, it was strange to see young foreigners in Japan who were not in uniform. I told him I was a missionary preparing to hold a tent crusade in town. This news seemed to excite him. He then told me he, too, was a Christian and would help our campaign if he could. That night he attended our Gospel meeting and sat on the very

35

first row. After the service he asked me if there was anything that he could do for me. Almost without thinking, I blurted out, "I'd love to get on the base to the PX cafeteria." I was weary of a diet of rice every meal and craved a good American-style hot dog and chocolate milkshake. He laughed and the next day took me to the base where he treated me to American chow. Boy, that simple hotdog and milkshake were more satisfying than any meal I could have had at the White House!

The hardest meal for us Westerners was always breakfast. Never, while out in the ministry, did we see anything like fried eggs, toast, cereal, or pancakes. In Japan, a breakfast staple was a thin soup with anemic bits of dried fish floating around. In Taiwan a Chinese breakfast consisted primarily of "syi fan" which is a porridge made by adding water to the leftover rice from the previous evening meal, garnished with peanuts, particles of squid, and Chinese pickles.

To supplement our meager diet, in the evenings after the evangelistic meetings had ended, we would often seek out street vendors for some tasty noodles. A small bowl cost no more than a few cents. The chopsticks were never clean but in the interest of health we would dip them in boiling water before ingesting the snack. To prepare the utensils for the next customer, the vendor simply sloshed the bowl and chopsticks in a wooden bucket full of tepid gray water kept under the counter. Why every one of us did not die of hepatitis is still a mystery.

Another crusader for whom the diet occasioned extreme, serious and even life-threatening illness was Dick Amos. The paucity of palatable local fare tempted the foreign crusaders to seek various tasty snacks from candy bars to colorful local-baked goods. One morning Dick, after completing his rounds, headed back to the OMS campus. Passing a bakery en route, he spied a display of luscious pink cream puffs in the front window. The price was reasonable and the temptation just too much. Purchasing three of the enticing pastries, he hastily consumed them before heading to a nearby barbershop.

As the barber applied clippers and comb, Dick became aware of a mild discomfort in his lower region, gradually intensifying until it produced a gastric discomfort far worse than any nausea he had ever experienced. In a moment he was forced to flee the barber chair and head for an open window. Hanging practically prostrate over the window sill, fortunately unobstructed by bars or screen, he began to disgorge the contents of his stomach. Things got worse. Loud gagging was followed by convulsions without remittance. With a word of apology, Dick exited the barbershop and stumbled several blocks to the OMS Bible school campus and the Dyers' home where he was being housed. By this time, the gagging had given way to vomiting blood. Dick, an athletic Texan, who had always been reticent to ask for help now made his condition known to OMS missionaries who immediately rushed their patient to the hospital. There, doctors diagnosed Dick's illness as food poisoning and applied emergency remedies. By morning, Dick was well enough to return to the campus, weak but grateful he had survived.

In fact, Dick's ordeal was far from over. A short time later this disgustingly healthy, young man gave symptoms of a malady worse than food poisoning—a debilitating weakness accompanied by an alarming change of skin color. It was indeed the dreaded yellow jaundice or hepatitis. The doctor prescribed that he must lie perfectly still without labor or movement of any kind. This he attempted to do for an interminable three months, "the longest months of my life!" Afterwards he gingerly returned to his crusade team and sedulously avoided street food and the enticements of Japanese baked goods and the sweets which daily beckoned to hungry young Americans.

Perhaps more than anyone else, Frank Davis, the first volunteer of the second crusade, experienced in illness the greatest test of faith. He wrote:

I had not been in Japan long before I became ill with infectious hepatitis, probably due to the diet. Struggling to keep going with this serious illness, I became extremely discouraged. I could not understand God's purpose in allowing that debilitating sickness. Why had God ordained that I should be sick for what turned out to be three-quarters of the time I was in Japan? But the Lord used me in spite of the obstacles, and I saw many souls won to Him. Due to my condition which forced me to stay in Tokyo most of the time, I was able to use past training and experience to help in the mission's financial and organizational programs. On the return boat trip from Japan, the Lord met me in a wonderful way with His Holy Spirit again filling me. I rededicated my life to Him. After marrying Martha Dennis, a truly devout and wonderful lady, and following my seminary graduation, we returned to Japan where we spent the next 40 years.

Chapter 11

ROAD HAZZARDS

During the crusade when the teams were transferred from one location to another, they were usually provided a truck or a sort of van called a carryall. At this time few Japanese had cars so it was usually the Western missionary with a driver's license who was the chauffeur. Traffic in those days was haphazard at best and, to complicate things, in Japan, cars are driven on the left side of the road. Some of the greatest trials of the young crusaders related to vehicles. The narrow rutted country roads left a great deal to be desired and precipitated all sorts of car trouble. Charles Kempton, from eastern Ohio, who later went as a missionary to Brazil, tells of a memorable experience:

I was traveling alone on a country road when suddenly the carryall stopped. I tried to start it but the tired, old vehicle emitted only a growl. I got out to check the engine but could find nothing wrong. I opened the trunk to get my tool box but to my dismay discovered that the day before, when I had been working on another vehicle, I had forgotten to return the tools to my car. I tried again to start it but no go. What a helpless feeling, I'll tell you, being stranded far out in a rural area without a telephone or any means of relaying my discomfiture to any of my other teammates or missionaries. I tried again and again to start that old vehicle but to no avail. I knew there was no easy way to get help. Two buses a day passed going toward my destination and both had already gone. I stopped, calmed myself, and then prayed, "Lord, what should I do?" To my surprise He spoke to me very clearly. He said, "Chuck, don't you know I am the great mechanic?" I hesitated. I had trusted God for many things but had never thought of Him working on a car. In my desperation, I finally prayed, "God, give me a small miracle." I then climbed back in the carryall, turned the key, and pressed the starter. Immediately the old vehicle rumbled to life. That miracle provision on a desolate country road will remain forever a blessed reminder of my Lord's faithfulness.

Crusader Leslie Herbert from Great Britain describes another highway adventure:

By midday, January 19, 1956, our team had completed their distribution assignment and was ready to move to another location. It was lunch time so we dined on cold rice, fish, and fruit. We then loaded the carryall and began our journey. Our route took us along the edge of a peninsula with the sea on one side and a steep mountain rising on the other. It was a beautiful scene, albeit a very narrow road. Suddenly coming toward us loomed a large transport truck. The driver was occupying far more than his share of the road. I found myself in a dilemma. On my right was the steep embankment and on my left about 30 feet below were huge rocks and angry breakers. As the big truck approached, I realized that something must my done. Slacking speed a little, I eased to the left edge of the road in order to allow the truck to pass. But in so doing I hit a surprisingly soft shoulder. Before I knew it the earth had given way under my left wheel, and I was unable to bring the vehicle back onto the road. In fact, our car was now riding on two wheels and threatening to plunge perilously down into the ocean about 25 feet below. A moment later it happened. The carryall pitched over the edge and began to roll over and over toward the sea and crashing breakers. Without a doubt, I thought to myself, we are doomed and will end up in the water and could even drown.

I must confess at this point my life-long faith in God's deliverance was in jeopardy! I remembered that earlier that morning we had sung, "With Jesus I Can Safely Go," followed by the words, "knowing I shall wake never more to roam." Now at this moment "waking never more" was not a particularly comforting thought. Then with a very violent bump, the car stopped rolling and came to an abrupt halt. I anticipated that the sea would pour into the car and we would all be swimming for our lives. But no, none of these imagined disasters followed. I cautiously looked around and realized that we were grounded, safe and sound.

Incredibly the vehicle was upright on its wheels and the water still some distance away. I checked on my companion and found that he had somehow been transferred from the front seat to the back. He lay half buried by baggage and stacks of literature. My first question in Japanese, one of the few Japanese sentences I could actually say correctly was, "How are you? Are you all right?" When he answered in the affirmative, I was almost too stunned to say "praise the Lord." This was indeed an astounding miracle that God had wrought for us. Of course the car was very badly damaged but, in time, it was repaired and we were on the road again.

When I (EE) arrived in Taiwan in September 1958 to continue the crusade initiated by Lowell Williamson several years earlier, our team inherited an ancient red Ford pickup truck with a locally constructed body, seating eight, with six perched on benches in the truck bed. Apparently funds were not sufficient to equip the old vehicle with respectable tires. They were very nearly bald and road conditions terrible. Our journeys usually featured at least one flat for every trip of any distance. To add to our woes, the ancient jack was only occasionally in working condition. The next two years we often repeated our favorite verse in James 1: "Consider it pure joy, my brothers, whenever you face trials of many kinds."

In the fall of 1959, our team moved to the east coast of Taiwan to plant our first church in the sizable city of Hualien. This required packing ourselves and baggage into the old red truck for that journey which was a challenge indeed. The arrival of typhoon season had all but destroyed 100 miles of the precipitous and rutted east coast highway from Taitung to Hualien. En route we learned that this last stretch of road was now considered impassable. Since for our crusades a vehicle was indispensable, both for human transportation and carrying luggage and equipment, it was finally decided that five of our team members would make the final leg by train. My interpreter, Joseph Wang, and I would attempt to make the trip in the red truck. Rain and wind had destroyed large portions of the highway, washed away bridges and wreaked the sort of destruction for which these storms are famous.

As we commenced our journey, we prayed with a sincerity of historic proportions and continued to anoint every mile of the highway with perpetual intercession. On that road, ten mph would be considered a reckless speed. Where bridges had been destroyed, I drove into rivers the depth of which we had no way of gauging. Villagers along the way encouraged us with the information that the road ahead was ruined and our journey would likely end in disaster. Foolishly and prayerfully, I drove on.

Early in the afternoon, we were gratified to discover that the highway was improving. Just ahead of us, the dark red soil of the broadening concourse invited me to hasten our journey in order to reach our destination before dark. As we ascended a steep embankment, it occurred to me that the stretch of road on the other side of the undulating highway was totally obscured. On an impulse, I jammed on the brake and the vehicle skidded to a halt. There directly ahead of our front wheels was a precipice where the highway had totally washed away. We finally found an alternating road and traveled on reaching Hualien at dusk. Joseph and I were uttering prayers, this time of profound thanksgiving.

Some weeks later a letter from Mother informed me that during the night she had been awakened, suddenly impressed to pray for her son. It was on the very day of our memorable journey.

Chapter 12

OUR "ENEMY"

From the outset of the second crusade in 1950, it had been stated that the primary goal would be to once more place the Word of God and the plan of salvation in every home in Japan. This had been gloriously achieved in 1918, thanks in part to the heroic ten young men from God's Bible School. Now the feat was to be repeated by young men of a new generation and a new era. Our admiration for those early crusaders grew as we attempted to repeat their accomplishments. Japan is a country of many islands and dominated by high mountains of which Mt. Fuji is the queen. Our daily treks took us miles into the hinterlands, down ravines and up slopes, along narrow foot paths to remote locations where perhaps only two or three huts were perched on a steep hillside. We were usually teamed with one of our national colleagues due to our language limitations. Where there seemed to be interest in the Gospel, our partner would take over, asking questions and inviting the residents to attend our service that night. As a result many came and a good number were saved.

It must be admitted that in time the initial goal of literally reaching every home gave way to a somewhat different strategy. This called for residence in a town until there was a nucleus of believers, enough to start a church when the team moved on. One of our number would then stay behind to pastor the infant congregation.

Early on, we also discovered the Japanese' fervent desire to learn English, and teaching them our language became an effective means of making friends and leading students to Christ. During the 1913 – 1918 crusade, Japanese had a powerful curiosity and desire to meet the foreigners who had come to their community. Many had never before seen a European. Now 50 years later with many servicemen in the area, the sight of Americans was not unusual. GIs here as elsewhere had developed a reputation for friendliness and generosity. Some had even married Japanese. Of course, servicemen would also have a reputation for questionable morality, and crusaders were frequently approached by attractive geisha types with something other than religion on their minds.

Many of the early crusaders had very little, if any, prior contact with Japanese. They had questions derived from the terrible epithets so common in World War II. These described the "Japs" as a savage and blood-thirsty people, haters of the United States and instigators of the cruel attack on Pearl Harbor, who were bent on our destruction. To their surprise, however, upon arriving in Japan and familiarizing themselves with the gentle people, the young Americans soon formed a very different opinion. Crusader Ray Huey said, "I was amazed to find the Japanese people polite, clean, industrious, smart, zealous in religious faith (Shinto and Buddhist), and amazingly peace loving." Students of history insist that a very small percent of the Japanese population had any desire to go to war with the U.S. in 1941, and Japan's entry into that conflict was instigated by a small cadre of militarists who, over the objections of their colleagues, had virtually hijacked the nation.

After the bombing of Hiroshima and Nagasaki, the Japanese were expecting the Americans to be a savage people, determined to wreak retribution on a people who had bombed Pearl Harbor and invented Kamakazi attacks to destroy Americans.

The impression that General MacArthur made, governing the nation with true Christian compassion and instigating all kinds of wise reforms, are to this day remembered with gratitude. In fact, Japanese came to almost worship the great general. They lined the street every morning and afternoon to pay their respects when MacArthur arrived at his office and returned home.

Chapter 13

COMRADES

Most of the crusaders' interpreters and Japanese associates had suffered terribly during the war years, many because of their faith and their refusal to worship the emperor or to join in the Kyodon, the government-controlled church, which consisted of all of the denominations merged into one body. In the crusade we were privileged to work with pastors who had lost their church buildings by fire or bombs. During the war their congregations had been scattered and many pastors found themselves out of a job. OMS now put them to work in the ECC ministry. This meant that our partners were trained pastors and evangelists, godly men with a passion for evangelism. In the words of one crusader, "I soon realized I was out of my league. These were experienced men and Christian stalwarts. I was still a neophyte, yet I did have a role to play."

Lowell Williamson, who had arrived in Japan in 1952, soon learned that his colleagues expected him to be a young Billy Graham and preach with vigor several times a week. He recalls:

> Most of us foreign crusaders had done very little if any preaching and the prospect of speaking in a foreign land was quite intimidating, to say the least. One blessing, however, was that our interpreters were almost all experienced preachers. I remember that the first time I stood behind the pulpit it was with fear and trembling and the certainty that I would do a very poor and inadequate job. But to my amazement when the interpreter put my words into Japanese the message came out with great

eloquence and conviction resulting in many staying afterwards to receive Christ as Savior.

Some of the interpreters admittedly knew very little English and actually understood less than half of what the American crusaders were saying. This did not inhibit them in the least. They proceeded to preach with great eloquence. Dick Amos remembers one of his first messages. His beloved teammate and interpreter was Brother Okamura. This is the man most often referred to by the young crusaders as the greatest inspiration to them personally, a man who during the war had suffered persecution beyond measure and once very nearly died under torture.

Dick remembers in the early summer of 1959:

> Our team was led by Okamura Sensei (sensei is the honorific word for mister, gentleman or sir). My first turn to speak came a few days after the campaign began. That night I preached on "Why Jesus died for you" with Okamura interpreting. There were about 45 or 50 people in attendance. At the close we gave an invitation. I was awed to see the expressions on the faces of our listeners. As was customary we asked those who wanted to believe in Jesus as their Savior to raise their hands. Quickly 20 hands went up. Amazed, I concluded that my audience had misunderstood what I had said. I turned to Okamura and asked, "Do you think they really understood?" "Oh, yes," he replied, "I'm sure they did." That night I realized that God was at work in Tateoka and in and through my dynamic interpreter, Okamura. He was a bold and powerful spokesman who could take my feeble and hesitant offering and transform it into a powerful and convicting message.

Another crusader, Grant Nealis, was an Asbury College graduate from Lexington, Kentucky. He and I (EE) had been roommates, and he would one day be the OMS field leader in Hong Kong. He recalls that:

> God used our team to build a church in the northern section of Nagoya city. He provided me with a wonderful interpreter, Komisan, perhaps the only worker who had a diploma from an elite "English school." Every day Komisan patiently taught me some of the language and customs of Japan. When he interpreted for me, he was truly inspired. This man had taught himself Greek and was later on the faculty of our OMS seminary as both interpreter and a Greek teacher. He also operated the school bookstore. What tremendous experiences I had serving God with that team. When I returned to Asbury Seminary, my professor of Christian Education, an old friend, said, "Grant, I don't know what you did for Japan but Japan surely did a lot for you!"

Another Asburian, Austin Boggan, a tall, handsome blond from Alabama, had also joined the crusade. After a year in Japan, he was asked to transfer to Korea where the war had recently ended. His assignment was to assist Elmer Kilbourne in many ways but particularly to help reconstruct the devastated churches in that land.

In Japan Austin had worked with the crusade team captain, Kobiyashi Sensei, and also Mori Sensei, the assistant team captain. Both of these men had been imprisoned in Japan during World War II because they refused to join the government church, which required an act of obeisance to the emperor. Boggan recalls

49

that "Kobayashi told me that he and other prisoners had prayed that the U.S. would win the war so that the Japanese would be free to evangelize their own people." Austin continues:

One of our team members was brother Tashurosan. He had been inducted into the military at age 13 and trained to be a kamikaze pilot. Thank God the war ended before he was called up. He was 22 when I had the privilege of winning him to Christ in a campaign led by evangelist Dwight Ferguson.

When we traveled on the Japanese trains, I would witness through my interpreter Brother Hedetakisan. As I preached, he would interpret. Being much shorter than I, he would stand up on a seat beside me and address the entire car. What a soul winner!

Another of our workers, Katosan, had been part of a cutthroat gang in Yokohama. One night, fed up with his life of violence and murder, he was on his way to commit suicide. His route took him past one of our Gospel tents where he heard singing and wandered into the meeting. That night he responded to the invitation and got saved. He spent the night with the team and asked to join us when we left the following day. We hired him as our cook for the next crusade after which he became a full-fledged crusader. When Christmas came, all the men went home except Kato. He returned to Yokohama where he met his old gang. Afraid he would now blow the whistle on them, they beat him up and for a time locked him in a room. Some weeks after the other crusaders had returned, Kato managed to escape and headed straight back to the crusade. He arrived, the victim of a terrible beating, dried blood on his torn clothes. He looked grotesque with half his head shaved but a triumphant smile lit his face. What a privilege it was for me to work with these heroes of the faith who were willing to literally lay down their lives for the sake of Jesus.

Kemp Edwards had a number of interpreters but for him the best remembered was also Okamura Sensei. During the war, this heroic man had been tortured for faith in Christ and his unwillingness to worship the emperor or to join the government church. Kemp says, "My Japanese partners taught me so much, especially challenging me with their knowledge of God's Word and their prayer lives. I know that rubbing elbows with them tremendously changed my life. I'm especially thankful for their patience with this 'gaijin' (foreigner) who did not have the gift of languages and struggled every day with the impossible Japanese tongue." Later Kemp, after finishing Asbury Seminary, married Jean Pratt and returned to Japan as a career missionary. They were stationed in the northernmost province of Hokkaido, where Kemp again had the privilege of working with his old friend, Okamura Sensei.

Stan Dyer was also deeply impressed by the prayer life of his Japanese colleagues, and he, too, for a time worked with Mr. Okamura of whom he says:

Very soon I saw the heart and passion of this man. He was a prayer warrior. Kneeling on the hard, straw-mat floor he would agonize with God for souls. His leadership impacted not only the Japanese to whom he ministered but also the lives of his team members, including my own. Later Reverend Gempachi Saito, another godly brother, was assigned to my team. This semi-retired pastor was short in stature but tall in spiritual passion. He often spent hours in fervent intercessory prayer. Later his son became pastor of the Kobe church, the very church I had helped plant. His grandson also studied for the ministry and is currently associate pastor of the OMS seminary church in Higashi-muriama.

Chapter 14

"CAN'T YOU TELL US NOW?"

Stanley Dyer tells of his first days in the crusade and the beginning of the Gospel distribution program:

Upon my arrival in Japan in 1956, I was assigned to work with a team of Japanese men in the Hiyogo prefecture. At that time, just over 10 years since the war had ended, the dwellings in farming communities were still very primitive. Most of the rural homes were small, thatched-roof cottages with paper doors and windows. Country roads were narrow dirt or gravel paths through expanses or plots of farmland and forests. Our goal was to visit every home in the area and give all residents a booklet, "The Way of Peace." As we visited in doorways, we would explain the story of Christ who could give inner peace to the searching hearts of Japanese. When possible we held evangelistic meetings in the local community halls or in a tent that we would pitch on a vacant lot.

In our distribution campaign, if feasible, we would use our grey van, then known as a carryall. With me at the wheel, we would go bumping and swaying up and down narrow mountain paths. In one area the road consisted of two parallel paths that eventually reached a plateau and entered a small village, set back among stands of bamboo. The small mountain town consisted of some 100 thatched or tile-roofed homes. As usual we visited every home and explained the message of the Bible booklet. Whenever possible our team members would speak personally with every one they met, explaining the peace and joy that comes through faith in Jesus.

I remember one small village we came to where some inquired of our Japanese teammates, "Why is the foreigner with you?" and "What does he want?" My partner explained that I was helping them bring some very special news to the people of the village. One villager responded, "Can't you tell us the good news now? Why wait till tomorrow?" We then informed them that we would have a meeting in the community building that very evening.

The northern Japanese did not know much about Christianity or its teaching of Christ's promise of resurrection to all believers. They were eager to hear this new doctrine that was spreading in the lower islands. Stan remembers that:

One day as I passed out the pamphlet, "The Way of Peace," at a country farmhouse, an elderly lady of 81 years invited me to come into the house to talk. She explained that the rest of the family were out in the fields working. With tears in her eyes, she started to tell me that just that morning one of her grandchildren had said, "Granny, when are you going to die? You are a real burden to us. Another mouth to feed." I felt it was God's timing that had brought me to her home that day and caused her to unburden her troubled heart to a stranger. The message of God was truly good news for one convinced that no one really cared for her. God was also helping me in my imperfect Japanese to share His goodness and love with this dear soul. Before I left, I asked if I could pray for her. "Yes," she replied eagerly, "I would like you to pray." I prayed in English but the Spirit of God knit our hearts and spirits together in a very real and unmistakable way.

Kelly Toth, a young Canadian of Hungarian ancestry and a graduate of Roberts Wesleyan College, remembers that one day their distribution took them to the hot springs resort of Asami. In this remote area, few of the people had ever seen a foreigner in person. Here God used recent tragedies to focus attention on the uncertainty of life and man's need to prepare for eternity. Two well-known citizens of the community had died. The first was a teenage boy from one of the well-known families in town. The second was a woman who was tragically burned to death in her home.

Kelly says, "Of course, trying to minister with our very limited Japanese was always frustrating." The students of Asian languages are always bewildered by the many similar-sounding words with totally different meanings.

Kelly Toth tells of God's clear leading during Gospel distribution in a remote region:

> The next crusade campaign was outside the town of Asami where I sensed the clear leading of God. It was a bleak December day. The sharp winter wind whipped across my face as I pushed my way through the area. I had gone from one farmhouse to another for a number of hours. Big trucks passed me on the dirt road covering me with clouds of dust.
>
> I was tired and it was past time for me to head back for supper and prepare for the evening service. But as I turned around, I felt a strong inner urge to go a little farther. I had

earlier learned to obey these impressions and so I turned back to visit more homes. The very next house was a small, ramshackle Japanese dwelling. The occupants were obviously extremely poor. I greeted them with the usual "gomen kudoshi" and gave them the Gospel pamphlet, as well as a flyer inviting them to our services. Here, too, due to the cold, instead of using a tent we rented a building for our meetings. The next night a ragged farmer appeared at our Gospel hall and asked for me, "the American." Immediately I recognized him as Omura San, the same farmer whom I had visited the previous afternoon when I had felt the Spirit's prompting.

The service touched him deeply and he responded to the invitation to come forward to pray for forgiveness of sins. That night he accepted the Gospel and committed himself to Jesus Christ as Savior. Words fail me to describe the miraculous transformation that came to that simple man. Omura San then returned home with the Gospel story and the witness of a changed life.

The following night he was back at our meeting with his family. He gradually related how poverty had stalked him at every turn. The meager living he was making from the land was hardly sufficient to keep him and his family alive. "Why can we not be as successful as others?" his wife demanded. Their home was a daily scene of anger and blame. It was this that finally drove the man to despair.

For days he had sought for a way of escape and finally in desperation he decided to end his life. There seemed no alternative. It was at that very time that I had felt the Spirit of God prompting me to go a little farther.

The man carefully read the tract I'd given him. The words of hope suggested that there might be a solution for his misery. And there was, for God had given His son Jesus for man's salvation. Before long I received the following letter from him. "I heartily appreciate that you brought a bright light into my home the other day. I have been hoping for a long time that someone might lead me to God but no one did until you came to my house. I plan to go to Asami church with my children every Sunday. All hearts of my family members now are united in Christ and full of joy. We are trying to become fine Christians saturated with the Spirit of Christ."

Chapter 15

UNTO EVERY CREATURE

Hudson Hess was a recent graduate of Roberts Wesleyan College in Houghton, New York. He explains the origin of a very special love God gave him for the Japanese people. Strangely it was the fruit of his childhood experiences in the Philippines. Immediately after Pearl Harbor, Japanese armies had occupied the Philippines, imprisoning the entire Hess family who were missionaries there. Hudson recalls that "my father often counseled us children not to hate the Japanese for they did not know our Lord and Savior Jesus Christ. He also said that should our lives be spared we had an obligation to serve Him. Thus I knew in my heart then I was to become a foreign missionary and very possibly preach the Gospel to our former enemies in Japan." The ministry of Gospel distribution had a profound effect upon his life. He reports:

During scripture distribution in the mountains of northern Hyogo, we worked in a little community located in an Alps-like valley known in Japanese as "the eagles nest." It didn't take long to discover that these people had literally never heard the name of Jesus. That evening most of the village came together to hear the Gospel for the first time. They asked questions and stayed late into the night. Knowing that after we were gone, there was no one in the area to shepherd this little group we gave them the number of a radio station where they could find Gospel messages in their own language. This was the moment I truly understood the importance of Christian radio, and I determined to make the propagation of the Gospel by radio the goal of my life. We later served for years in Haiti with the OMS radio station, 4VEH, which reaches most of the Caribbean.

Another crusader, Charles Kempton, remembers:

One day doing Gospel distribution, we went to a little town 12 miles south of Meto. Most of the team members traveled by bicycle to assigned areas around the town while my interpreter, Mr. Okamura, and I covered the town. Making my way down the main north-south street, I noticed a stand of bamboo trees lining the creek. I thought I was at the town's edge since there were no signs of houses beyond the bamboo. However, as I approached the last house on the street, I happened to peer through a small hole in the wall and saw a thatched roof in the distance. Then I noticed a bridge across the stream and a path leading to four houses. In the last house, a young man responded to my greeting when I said, "This is a Christian book. Please read it." His eyes widened as he asked, "Are you a Christian?" I assured him I was. My simple reply unleashed a sudden torrent of words and emotion. With my limited Japanese, I could understand very little so I called my teammate to interpret.

With the help of Brother Okamura, I heard the following story: The young man it seems had long hungered for assurance of a home in heaven. He was told that the best way was to enlist in the army and die for the Divine Emperor. He did join the army and tried but failed to find an acceptable way to die. The Emperor's power couldn't save Japan from defeat. Hence, he reasoned, that America's God must be the true diety and thus began a quest for a Christian, someone to tell him about America's

God. He had been searching, he said, ten years for a Christian. He had recently written in response to an ad from the Japan Bible Society and received a free New Testament. He started at the beginning with Matthew but couldn't make sense of the genealogy so the New Testament was placed on his god shelf with other sacred items.

That day we were able to show him God's plan of salvation from his own copy of the New Testament. He opened his heart like a spring flower opens to the sun and claimed Christ as His savior. The next night he rode his bicycle 12 miles to share his testimony in our evening meeting.

Hudson also tells of a campaign in the town of Nishiwuaki:

This town was noted for its textile mills. A large number of young girls with sallow complexions filled the tent each night during the campaign. Praise God many of those lost sheep entrusted their lives to the Good Shepherd. One of the girls had run away from home. After receiving Jesus, she wrote to her family telling them of her whereabouts. They requested her to return home. Later when we visited her, we found that she was conducting children's meetings in her neighborhood, leading little ones to Jesus.

Stan Dyer tells of another memorable campaign:

In one town, we had difficulty finding a place to pitch the tent. We finally discovered an open yard. At one end was a tall building which was actually a temple. At the top of a long flight of steps stood a huge statue of Buddha. Our team leader had, with very little warning, advised me that I was to be the preacher that night. My pulpit would be situated atop the stairs directly in front of the great idol. When our meeting began, I felt like Paul preaching on Mars Hill with the Parthenon behind him. I stood a moment looking out over my congregation. More than 150 people had gathered to hear the news which this foreigner had brought to their village. It was certainly an intimidating situation for a 21-year-old greenhorn missionary. What should I say? How could I express the joy and peace in my heart? How could I help them understand the wonderful story of Jesus? I breathed a silent prayer for wisdom.

I then began with a brief greeting: "Good evening. We have come in peace with a very wonderful message." The people nodded as Brother Okamura interpreted and gave them appropriate Japanese greetings. I then asked, holding up my English Bible, "How many of you have ever seen a Bible? This is God's book. If you have seen this book, please raise your hand." No hands were raised, not one. This entire village had been totally without the message of God's grace. Then I asked a second question, "How many of you have heard the name Jesus Christ? Please raise your hands." It was a sobering moment. I paused, looked across the sea of faces and realized that not a single one of these had ever heard of my wonderful Savior. What should I say? How could I explain? This message would need to be both simple and clear. I then read from John's Gospel, chapter 3, verse 16. I will never ever forget the look of bewilderment on the faces of those 150 souls who expressed their total lack of knowledge either about the Word of God or the name Jesus Christ. It dawned on me that they were hearing the Gospel for the first time in their lives.

Evening tent service

Carryall loaded and ready to travel – 1953

Hudson Hess and admirer

Children's service

Prayer Reminder
for
YOUR CRUSADER
in

FORMOSA

Ed Erny

"Ye have not chosen me, but I have chosen you and ordained you, that ye should go and bring forth fruit and that your fruit should remain." John 15:16

The Oriental Missionary Society

HOME ADDRESS:
850 North Hobart Boulevard
Los Angeles 29, California

FIELD ADDRESS:
P. O. Box 74
Taichung, Taiwan (Formosa)

Prayer Reminder
for
OUR REPRESENTATIVE
in

KOREA

J. B. Crouse

"Therefore will I give thanks unto thee, O Lord, among the heathen, and sing praises unto thy name." Psalm 18:49

WORLD RELIEF COMMISSION
of the N. A. E.

HOME ADDRESS:
1219 Jackson Avenue,
Long Island City 1, New York

FIELD ADDRESS:
35-3 Ka
Choong Jung Ro
Seoul, Korea

Crusader Prayer Cards

Please Pray For

YOUR CRUSADER

to

JAPAN

Hudson Hess

"Go ye therefore, and teach all nations, baptizing them in the name of the Father, and of the Son, and of the Holy Ghost: Teaching them to observe all things whatsoever I have commanded you: and, lo, I am with you alway, even unto the end of the world."

Matt. 28:19 - 20

The Oriental Missionary Society, Inc.

850 North Hobart Blvd. Los Angeles 29, Calif.

Please Pray for

YOUR CRUSADER

to

JAPAN

Kelly Toth

Call unto me, and I will answer thee. and shew thee great and mighty things which thou knowest not.
Jeremiah 33:3

HOME ADDRESS
The Oriental Missionary Society
850 N Hobart Blvd.
Los Angeles 29, California

FIELD ADDRESS
391 Kashiwagi Cho
3 Chome, Shinjuki-ku
Tokyo, Japan

Crusader Prayer Cards

Stan Dyer and friends

Grant Nealis

Hudson Hess and Crusade partners

Dunbar, Dyer, Toth, and Hess with teammates

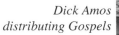

Dyer and Hess savor a radish

*Dick Amos
distributing Gospels*

Amos in kimono

Dyer, Nealis, Art Shelton, and Dunbar with team members in Nagoya

*Dale Neff aboard
the Andrew Jackson*

*Stan Dyer –
children's meeting*

Ed Erny,
Yuan Lin, Taiwan – 1959

Kemp Edwards

Erny and Edwards travel on the Laura Maersk

Crusaders Hess, Dunbar, Nealis, Herbert, and Dyer

Dyer: "Please take and read."

J.B. Crouse and Kilbournes, a meeting handbill

Elmer and Ella Ruth Kilbourne   J. B. Crouse, Jr.

Elmer Kilbourne Family and J. B. Crouse, Jr.

KOREA-BOUND

Elmer and Ella Ruth Kilbourne and daughters, Diane and
Pamela, will leave Los Angeles on September 8 for Seoul,
Korea after a furlough period in the States.

* * * * * * * * * * * * * * * * * * *

J. B. Crouse, Jr. (son of Rev. and Mrs. J. Byron Crouse,
Wilmore, Kentucky) will also leave on September 8 for
Korea, where he will begin his work as a first-term missionary. He will be in charge of supervising the N.A.E.
relief program in South Korea.

O.M.S. MISSIONARY RALLY

The ORIENTAL MISSIONARY SOCIETY HEADQUARTERS CHAPEL
850 North Hobart Blvd.   Los Angeles 29, California

SUNDAY, SEPTEMBER 7, 1958 - 2:30 P.M.

Virgil Dunbar and team

Mapping area for Gospel distribution

Austin Boggan assists in Korea food distribution

Crusade "buddies" – Dyer, Toth Hess, and Dunbar

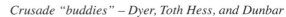

Crusade baptism

Virgil Dunbar

Dyer, children's meeting

Hess and teammates

Dyer, Hess, and team, loaded carryall

Dyer and Ernie Kilbourne, to Okinawa

Chapter 16

DAYS OF HARVEST

For OMS the early 1950s were unquestionably years of great harvest in Japan. The pages of *The Standard* abound with stories of many who were finding Christ in the nightly evangelistic meetings. Following the first full year of the crusade, 1951-52, the following statistics appeared in *The Standard*:

No. 1: Covering a period of 22 months, approximately 500,000 Gospels and tracts have been distributed to this same number of homes by our crusade teams.

No. 2: Approximately 17,000 men, women and girls have sought the Lord for salvation.

No. 3: Thirty-three new groups of believers have been organized into churches during this period and are meeting in regular worship services. Twenty-eight groups have also been added to already established churches.

And then: $50 will cover the approximate cost of one campaign.

This spiritual hunger was attributed to several factors. First, the soil had been prepared by a great deal of concentrated prayer, not only by the crusaders themselves but also by an army of supporters in the homeland, who promised to intercede for the young men and the campaigns. In most of the meetings, there was an unusual sense of the presence and power of the Holy Spirit. Large numbers of seekers came forward for the wonderful salvation to which they had just been introduced.

Secondly, there existed in Japan at this time a religious vacuum, occasioned by the nation's crushing defeat and humiliation of World War II. Japan, Korea and Taiwan all were beginning the slow process of rebuilding after the devastation. Not only had the "divine" Sun Emperor failed, he had confessed to the nation that he was not divine. Added to this was the sheer desperation of a people who were struggling to live on about a dollar a day. All this had created an eagerness to learn of any source of help, divine or otherwise.

Sad to say, in later years as the nation began to recover and, in time, prosper and enjoy the fruits of their wealth, the earlier interest in things spiritual gave way to an obsession with materialism and the pagan delights of the flesh. During the crusade, however, there existed without a doubt a mentality which reasoned that since the gods of Japan had been humiliated and crushed by the foreign powers, particularly the United States, logically it must follow that the God of the Western people must be superior. This was indeed a season of the sort which Christ described when He said, "Lift up your eyes and look on the fields for they are white already unto harvest."

In a *Standard* article, crusade leader Rolland Rice wrote: "This has been a glorious campaign with a glorious new church and at least 40 born-again people worshipping there. All this has occurred within the short space of only six weeks. We are praying and believing God to duplicate this miracle again and again in the days to come."

Crusader Dale Neff in an article in *The Standard* titled, "Their Testimonies Glistened like Jewels," wrote:

> We were holding meetings in Yorii, a good-sized town on the edge of the mountains. God came in power. The night I was to preach God burdened me with a message concerning the resurrection. Three wonderful Christian

64

high school girls from one of our other churches had been coming nights to witness and help us pray. This night their testimonies truly sparkled like jewels. As I preached, I felt a wonderful thrill as truths came to us from the Word. As we closed, we asked those who wanted to receive Jesus to raise their hands. Immediately hands went up all over the hall. Then I asked them all to come to the front for prayer. Eleven responded, all adults.

One night a grandmother, 87 years of age, attended. She told us that her home in Tokyo had been burned down during the war. Though she was very poor, she managed to build a small shack and lived there in poverty. "During this period," she related, "I began to worship all kinds of idols. Never once did I receive help or assurance of an eternal home in heaven. I came to the conclusion that it wasn't possible to have eternal life, and I wanted to die because I was getting too old to live. The first night I attended these meetings, I heard God's voice speaking to my soul. I had never heard that voice before, but I knew it was God. I began to worship Him immediately. From that time on, I gave up all my idols and trusted only in Jesus Christ. He cleansed my heart and right now I know that if I die I will live forever with Him." My interpreter asked, "Grandma, what about dying? Do you still want to die?" "Oh, I want to live now," she smiled. "I want to live till at least 90. I thank God He allowed me to live long enough to hear the Gospel and be saved."

Kemp Edwards tells of a tent campaign his team held in Akita city:

The attendance was one of our largest with 45 adults and 100 or more in youth meetings. One of the seekers was a young high school student who said he had been searching for salvation for two years. Under great conviction he awoke one night at about 2 a.m. Opening his Bible, he read Psalm 51 and was deeply moved. He attended our tent meetings night after night, finally yielding himself completely to the Lord Jesus Christ.

Chuck Dupree remembers an early campaign in Chiba, a prefecture town in greater Tokyo:

One evening a young man showed up outside our tent. He told us that he was interested in knowing more about Jesus. A team member, Mr. Ouchi, led him to Christ, and we could sense the wonderful joy that he had found. Mysteriously, however, the youth never returned for the evening services. We closed the campaign and moved to another town. There to our delight was the young man. He explained why he had not returned. This was his story.

One night his father had asked him to go on an errand. On the way he passed our tent. He heard the singing of "What a Friend we have in Jesus" and paused briefly to listen. Then he hurried on to take care of business. On the way back, he went slowly by the tent so he could hear what was being said. For the next several nights he continued to return. He would walk slowly up and down the street, listening to the message. Finally he got enough courage to come inside. This was the night brother Ouchi met him and led him to Christ. He was overjoyed but he knew that he dared not tell his father who was a stone mason. They worked together and his job was to bring his father stones

66

from the mountains to be carved into gods to sell to the people of the community. The problem our new convert now found was that he couldn't hide the change God had wrought in his life or the sheer joy. Finally his father asked why he was so different. Courageously, the young man told him that he had become a Christian and could no longer worship idols. His father was outraged. He picked up a large knife and shouted, "If you don't denounce your faith, I'll kill you."

The young man fled into the forest for the night, and the next day went to another town and stayed there with his married sister. We invited him to stay with our crusade team, do odd jobs, and take care of the tent during the day while we were away doing distribution work. This he joyfully agreed to do. We watched him grow in the Lord. Before I left Japan, he had enrolled in our Tokyo Bible Seminary, taking a laymen's course in order to serve in his home church.

Chuck Dupree tells of a later campaign:

During the evening service, I noticed a young lady would come into the tent about the time the preaching started and then leave before the service was over. One evening as she stood to leave, we greeted her. This led to a long conversation. I learned that she was the daughter of a Buddhist priest and lived in a corner of the temple yard, very near to where we were holding services. She told us that she worked for the city office and had noticed us when we visited the municipal office. Curious, she began attending our meetings. Eventually she prayed the sinner's prayer, inviting Christ into her life.

Charles Kempton remembers:

Early in the Japan crusade, a boy testified that one afternoon while playing with his friends he heard a loudspeaker atop a truck announcing tent meetings at the park. Thinking it was a circus, he persuaded his friends to go with him, and they ended up attending the crusade every night. After the tent was gone, he continually begged his mother to tell him how much longer it would be till Sunday when he could attend Sunday School. He simply could not get enough of God and the Bible. Then the boy took sick. They thought it was food poisoning and soon realized he was dying. Although in great pain, instead of crying or screaming, he sang songs he had learned at church—"Jesus loves me" and "Rolled away, rolled away." This surprised and amazed everyone. After the boy's death, the neighbors said they had never witnessed anyone die with such peace. They had never heard of the home by the beautiful river. They wanted to know more. This led them to the nearby church where they, too, received Christ as Savior.

Chapter 17

SAVED FROM SUICIDE

Kelly Toth and his team worked on the northern island of Hokkaido. During that time, he reported the following:

One night we met a young man named Kodamasan, the only son of a farmer. His father wanted him to take over and run the farm. This was far from the boy's ambitions. He wanted to be a school teacher. One day he ran off and got a job on the main island in Tsujido. He worked for a local manufacturer who treated employees badly, sometimes paying them and sometimes not. Kodama tried to draw attention to this man's crimes but no one cared to listen. He then decided to resort to a common Japanese revenge measure—to kill himself on the premises of the factory and leave a note for the police, explaining his suicide. He procured a knife, slit both wrists, and thrust his arms in hot water to facilitate massive bleeding. He passed out but came to the next morning, his bloody wrists clotted. Wracked by a terrible headache, he went outside to get some fresh air. Just as he reached the gate, one of our crusade team members approached, passing out invitations to the tent meeting. Kodama came that night and was wonderfully converted. Every night for the rest of the meetings he brought other workers from the factory with him. Praise God! I later learned that this young man had become an OMS pastor and started a church in Hokkaido.

One day while engaged in tract distribution, crusader Chuck Dupree was used of God to save the life of a Japanese girl. He relates:

That evening I was returning from Zama. This required that I change trains at the big central Shinjuku station. As I stood on the platform waiting for the express, a train approached on the opposite track. Suddenly I noticed a woman crossing the tracks where I stood. Clearly she was intent on throwing herself in front of the train. She staggered forward and landed face down across the tracks. By this time the thundering train was only a short distance away. Without thinking, I jumped down and lifted her back unto the platform, barely averting the locomotive. I could easily have been the one killed but God preserved my life and hers. I have often thought of that desperate lady and pray that as her life was spared so also will her soul be saved.

Chapter 18

THE BIRTH OF MEN FOR MISSIONS

During the third year of our crusade efforts, we were visited by a well-known evangelist, Dwight Ferguson. He had come from the United States with Stanley Tam, his friend from Lima, Ohio. Tam was the owner of a prospering silver-reclaiming business. When Ferguson, who had never been abroad, yielded to the imprecations of OMS President Eugene Erny and agreed to visit OMS fields in Asia, he insisted that he must also take along his friend from Lima.

The fruit of that historic encounter in 1952 resulted in two epic events: Following his return to the U.S., Dwight attended the OMS convention at Winona Lake, Indiana, where he organized the first-ever Men for Missions organization. For 200 years, Ferguson pointed out, North American churches had all had women missionary societies. None, however, had ever had a men's missionary organization. He set about to organize one. Today great numbers of men are going to mission fields as a result of this movement begun in the heart of Dwight Ferguson. Secondly, Stanley Tam, in turn, was so deeply impressed with the vast needs of Asia and the effectiveness of the Every Creature Crusade that before he left Korea he made a vow to turn over his entire business to God to support mission crusades. Today, the Tam fund supports nearly 300 ECC teams in OMS fields. This is all detailed in his book, *God Owns My Business*.

Crusader Ray Huey describes what happened when Ferguson later returned to Japan to preach one of the early crusade campaigns. He recalls:

The meetings were well attended with Brother Dwight Ferguson preaching. He certainly spoke under the anointing of the Holy Spirit, and every night there was a harvest of souls in abundance. Many of these people had never heard the Gospel before but the Holy Spirit revealed to their hearts that this was the true and only way of salvation. After each message, those who wanted to be saved were asked to go to the tent where they could pray. Again and again the tent was full of seekers and personal workers.

Chapter 19

CRUSADERS IN KOREA

Although the primary thrust of the second Every Creature Crusade, like the first, focused on the great island empire of Japan, in time other OMS fields began requesting that the ECC program be initiated in their countries as well.

Elmer Kilbourne, the grandson of OMS founder, E.A. Kilbourne, had been raised in China and Korea. After completing his schooling at Asbury College and Seminary, he and his wife, Ella Ruth, had returned to China and Korea as missionaries. They had been in Seoul on black Sunday, June 1950, when the North Korean Communists swept down like an evil tide into the city, killing thousands of their fellow countrymen and executing hundreds of pastors. Before the war was over three years later, the entire country lay in ruins. Kilbourne remembers that one could hardly recognize a single building in Seoul. The city was nothing but a ghastly scene of ruin and rubble.

OMS began relief work in cooperation with the newly organized World Relief Commission. Elmer, a close friend of Bob Pierce actually initiated the founding of World Vision, opening orphanages and homes for street children, widows and even lepers. Elmer also supervised a feeding program which served more than 20,000 meals to refugees a day. Overwhelmed with this incredible load of responsibility, he requested that an OMS crusader be sent to aid him in the relief ministry.

When no candidate was immediately supplied, Elmer took it upon himself to recruit one. J.B. Crouse was the son of Byron Crouse, who with Eugene Erny and Virgil Kirkpatrick had undertaken the famous Asbury tour in 1929-31. All three men had come back with a permanent, lifetime commitment to missions. J.B., who had grown up in a home where missions was a prime subject, had upon graduation from Asbury College begun seminary. When Elmer Kilbourne arrived in the Crouse home for a brief visit, it occurred to him that J.B. might just be the perfect assistant for management of the huge feeding program. J.B. agreed to consider this invitation. He prayed, "Lord, if you'll furnish a wife to go with me and also provide my funding, I will help Elmer in Korea." Since a recent romance had fallen through, J.B. now had no immediate matrimonial prospects. The thought of traveling alone to a war-torn land for years did not appeal to him. "Then," he says, "the Lord spoke to me and said, 'J.B., if you don't obey me, you will miss a tremendous opportunity I have prepared for you.'"

So that September 1958, J.B. boarded a plane bound for Seoul, Korea, where he was to direct the daily distribution of food to vast numbers of refugees every day. Along with food, missionaries were also providing desperately needed clothing and medical care.

In the course of his labors, J.B. met Bette Ships, a fellow Asburian now teaching in the famous Severens Hospital. Bette's father, Dr. Hammel Ships, a noted surgeon, was then serving on the OMS board of directors. J.B. had known Bette in college but they had never dated. Now it became immediately clear that their growing friendship was part of divine providence. J.B. and Bette married and continued as missionaries in Korea for decades. J.B. was elected OMS president in 1991, a position that he held until his retirement in 2005.

Another young crusader to whom Elmer gave a Macedonian call was Austin Boggin, who at this time was a crusader in Japan. In the life story of Elmer Kilbourne entitled *Missionary Maverick*, he tells of an unforgettable experience with Austin in a typhoon off the coast of Korea. Austin remembers it well:

Our assignment that day was to purchase supplies for some of the churches now in the process of being rebuilt. Since roads were in poor condition, we decided it would be easier to travel to the depot by boat. Elmer had a small 12-foot craft used for this purpose. On July 5, 1954, we commenced what we thought would be a brief trip of 30 miles or so up the coast. Korea has some of the highest tides in the world and, by the time we started back, the tide was going out. There are also scores of reefs and low-lying islands along the coast that pose no hazard at high tide. When the tide goes out, however, negotiating this area by boat requires extreme caution.

On our return trip, we had not traveled far before a sharp report from under the boat informed us that we had hit one of the reefs. We were relieved, however, to discover that the impact had apparently done no real damage other than to dent the pan. It took us almost an hour to repair that. We then started the engine, prayed, and were on our way.

In time, however, we noticed something strange. We were using a great deal of gasoline, far too much, and no matter how much we pulled the throttle we could never attain any speed. Then to our dismay we found out that when we hit the reef it had also broken off the sediment bowl. Gas was steadily leaking out and in a short time was all gone. When we anchored our disabled craft, we calculated that we were no more than 200 yards from shore. No cause for concern. We were confident that we could find help in the morning. During the night, however, the wind began picking up. Soon our anchor line broke, and we found ourselves being driven due west, out into the Yellow Sea. With alarm we realized that we were indeed caught in a dangerous windstorm, known in the West as a hurricane and in Asia "a great wind" or typhoon. We sent up flares in an attempt to signal small Korean fishing craft in the area. None seemed to notice. We approached island after island but, as is characteristic in such waters, currents flow swiftly in circular paths around the islands, making it virtually impossible for a stricken craft to land.

The following day we spotted American search planes, but they remained at quite a distance. Our flares and signaling efforts to attract their attention all failed. The second night we were far from land and in the maw of a treacherous storm. We knew that this could be the end of our mission on earth. Still, strangely, my heart was amazingly calm knowing that I was ready to meet my Savior and likely very soon would be seeing Him face to face. Within hours or minutes, we could be entering our heavenly home. Never in all my life have I had such a sweet and peaceful feeling. I had often talked and preached about that hope we have in Jesus Christ, but this was the first time I had ever come face to face with what appeared to be imminent death.

But at the same time, there were troubling thoughts. I knew that my life and service to God on earth was likely ending. Could it be that my years of preparation for ministry and missionary work were now finished, after only a few months on the field? A prayer rose in my heart, "Lord, save me. Save me for service, not for self." Then gradually there flooded over me an uncanny assurance that somehow all would be well.

The storm, however, rather than abating grew worse, throwing up great mountains of water. We knew that our 12-foot boat could not possibly stay afloat much longer in this kind of a tempest. We sat there in the grip of those powerful waves that repeatedly swept us up to a crest and then dashed us downward, imparting the sensation that as a kid I had first experienced on a roller coaster ride. With each wave we beseeched God to keep the boat upright. As we survived each terrific breaker, we breathed a sigh of relief and then braced ourselves for the next one.

We now realized that we would very likely end up in China for we were steadily moving in that direction. And in view of the hostile relationship between China and the U.S. at that time, we would probably perish in a Chinese prison. We prayed as never before. It was 2 a.m. We were worn out from our efforts and also exhausted from hunger, exposure and thirst. We had been without food or water for two days. I cried, "Lord, man's hand is helpless without You. We can do nothing. Now, Father, give us a miracle."

Shortly, the prevailing winds changed and, instead of driving us on towards the China coast, they were sweeping us back towards Korea. Then for some strange reason, I felt good, relieved, hopeful. I thought, "This is the hand of God and He will get glory for our salvation." Two hours later we approached an island. This time instead of futilely circling it we were, with each circuit, drawn closer and closer. Strangely the island remained always directly ahead as though an unseen rudder was guiding us. As we strained our eyes, we could see vegetation that began to form a pattern. Now we could make out several small houses and finally the forms of people. The island was inhabited! We soon discovered that there were three families of fishermen who lived there.

Thirty minutes later we were close enough for island inhabitants to see our distress signals. An old man ran to a point high on the island, pulled off his shirt, and with it signaled for us to go around to the other side where the waves were not so high and where there were no boulders. This we attempted but the strong current thrust us toward a perilous, rock-strewn stretch of the coast. Now completely out of control, it was as though a huge hand was driving us straight toward massive boulders. The boat will certainly be smashed we thought and we will be killed. Then we noticed that there was a small opening between the great rocks about 15 feet wide. Amazingly the current suddenly caught our small boat, drove us straight through the opening and onto the shore. With the final impact of a huge wave, we were lifted out of the boat and deposited upright on the sandy beach. Spontaneous hallelujahs rose in our hearts.

The fishermen returned Elmer and Austin to the Korea mainland where they discovered that they had been given up for dead and preparations were being made for a memorial service which now was turned into a celebration of thanksgiving.

Following Austin's two years in Asia, he married his fiancée Nelda Rackliffe and the two of them went to Brazil as missionaries with OMS. Austin is now in his 80s and still involved in evangelism in South America. He says, "What can I do? I can find no stopping place."

As reports of the crusade in Japan were circulated throughout OMS, calls came from other fields. One of the first was Hong Kong.

Chapter 20

HONG KONG CRUSADES

In the early 1950s, following the Chinese Communist takeover, millions of refugees fleeing Mao's armies arrived in the British colony of Hong Kong. Florence Monroe, a widow who with her husband had earlier worked with OMS in Canton, saw in these displaced people a great opportunity for evangelism. She had mastered the Cantonese language and was greatly used of God to establish an OMS beachhead in Hong Kong, the most densely populated city in the world.

Apart from this great city, a British colony, the mainland of China was now entirely under Communist control. Although for a time missionaries were allowed to stay, almost all Christian work had come to a halt. Furthermore, it was becoming increasingly problematic for Chinese nationals to in any way be associated with foreign missionaries. By the early 50s, the China mainland, though not yet fast closed, was definitely behind the "bamboo curtain." Millions of Chinese, especially those in southern provinces, knew enough of Communism to determine that if at all possible they would not live under the dictatorship of Mao Tse-Tung. Beginning in 1948, throngs of refugees began arriving in Hong Kong. In time, defenses were built around the colony, but refugees still managed somehow to sneak past the barriers and evade the guards. Others found escape from China by the sea, boarding small crafts at night in Macao which was at the time a Portuguese colony. From there, they would surreptitiously sail or swim into Hong Kong under cover of darkness.

All this created tremendous problems for Great Britain and her prized show-place possession which for decades had been the most valuable piece of real estate in Asia. Now refugees, lacking adequate housing, spilled over into the streets. Huge numbers were sleeping on sidewalks. Others made a home on rooftops, in stairwells and attics. Hundreds of thousands erected flimsy wooden huts, creating shack villages perched on Hong Kong's tilted hillsides. The government eventually began to address the housing problem by erecting huge concrete block shelters, four stories high and assigning five refugees to a room. A forest of such buildings started to rise in Kowloon, the area of the city across the bay from Hong Kong Island.

Visiting the British Colony and witnessing the millions of desperate people without proper lodging, food or employment, Florence Munroe came away with a passion and a plea which she laid upon the directors of OMS. "The mission must, at all costs," she pled, "open a field in Hong Kong." Florence herself, now well past retirement age, volunteered to be OMS' first missionary to the colony. The field was opened in 1953. Florence was soon joined by Dale and Polly McClain, veteran OMSers, who had also served with her in Canton and spoke Cantonese. Following a term in India, the McClains returned to the teeming Cantonese-speaking city of Hong Kong to assist. New missionaries, Robert and Phyllis Erny, arrived soon after.

With millions of displaced refugees in the colony desperate for consolation and succor from any quarter, what better time to minister to both their physical and spiritual needs? All this combined to create a period of unprecedented harvest which in turn gave birth to scores of churches. In this crowded city, space was at a premium. Florence now noticed that the broad rooftops of the H-block refugee housing buildings were mostly unused.

81

Why not then send evangelistic teams into Hong Kong with schools and churches opened atop the flat-roofed buildings? Florence was not slow to visit British officials and acquire permission for the endeavor. This gave rise to a vision for crusade campaigns, both in the city as well as inland areas designated the New Territories. A call went out for Hong Kong crusaders.

The first crusader assigned to Hong Kong was Buddy Gaines. Buddy had been an outstanding leader at Asbury College and elected president of the student body. Despite a romance with an attractive Asbury coed, in 1960 he felt God calling him to the Hong Kong Every Creature Crusade where he joined a team of nationals. In the besieged colony, great numbers of displaced Chinese turned to Christ for comfort and salvation. In a *Standard* article, Buddy wrote:

> During our regular visitation and Gospel distribution program, we met a housewife, Mrs. Hoh. After a few minutes of conversation, she went into a back room and produced a folded newspaper. In it was one of our Gospel tracts with the OMS address stamped on the back. She said, "My husband received this the other night. We are tired of worshipping the false gods and ancestors. We want to know about the God called Jesus."
>
> She accepted our invitation to attend the evening service, and the following Sunday we rejoiced to see her and her husband in our Gospel Hall. In this first meeting they accepted Christ as Savior. Now they learned that they should give up their idols if they wanted to be true Christians. Would they be willing to do this? Would they actually abandon the religion of their people, their relatives and ancestors? For most Chinese this is an

exceedingly difficult decision and often brings upon them the reproach of their neighbors. But when we mentioned this to them, they told us that they already had made their decision and not worshipped idols for more than a week.

We went to their home the following Sunday afternoon. They lived in a rough-hewn wooden house, consisting of a small sitting room, bedroom and kitchen. In the rear was an odiferous enclosure where they raised pigs to augment their income. After being seated on low wooden stools, we opened the meeting with prayer and then the Gospel song, "There is power in the blood," followed by the Bible reading and a short message. Through my interpreter, I explained the purpose of the meeting and why it was necessary to tear down and destroy all of the family idols. We then proceeded to do just that, removing the ancestral shrine and family gods, taking them outside, and chopping them up.

At this point a neighboring teenager appeared, his face contorted with rage. He was carrying two large rocks and swearing that the gods would not forgive us for what we were doing. Mr. Hoh spoke to him firmly, but kindly, telling him that they did indeed know what they were doing. After the idols were destroyed, they were committed to the flames. Christ had won another victory.

Buddy and his assigned team not only took the Gospel to the throngs in the city proper but also into the rural areas located along the colony's extremities bordering on Communist China. His second year in Hong Kong, he assisted World Vision which was establishing a large facility for abandoned street boys.

After returning to the U.S., Buddy married his sweetheart, Marty Ewan, and completed seminary. The two of them returned to Hong Kong as missionaries. Later, after receiving training in James Kennedy's Evangelism Explosion (EEII), Buddy was seconded by OMS to EE and appointed its Asia director. He spent several decades traveling the world from Asia to areas of Eastern Europe and Russia, conducting scores of seminars and training thousands in the new and tremendously effective program of winning souls to Christ and growing churches.

Chapter 21

THE SECOND WAVE

In the mid 1960s, a second wave of Hong Kong crusaders arrived led by Billy Campbell, a zealous young man from the British Isles. Billy recalls:

> I first heard of the OMS crusade program at a meeting in Ireland led by OMS missionary from Taiwan, Doris Trefren. She handed us copies of *The Standard*. On the back cover was an appeal for ECC workers. This opened to my mind a new and exciting world of evangelistic opportunity. The ad read, "Do you want to know God's will? Are you willing to do God's will? Join the Every Creature Crusade in Hong Kong." Jim McKinstry, the OMS British Isles' director, suggested that before I go overseas I get some Bible training. This led me to enroll in a Bible college after which I applied to OMS for the crusade. Thus meeting one key person and seeing that ad on the back of the OMS magazine changed the whole direction of my entire life.

Following Billy's ECC term, he completed his Bible college degree and then returned to Hong Kong as a fulltime missionary. For a period, Billy and Jean, his wife, also served as the OMS British Isles director and then later as the director in Australia. They are now back in Asia in a ministry of evangelism and the training of Christian workers.

Another Hong Kong crusader was Duane Beals, a young man of unusual abilities and great drive. His assignment in Hong Kong forever fixed in him a missionary vision. He was later elected president of Western Evangelical Seminary in Portland, Oregon. Today he teaches at Bethel College in Indiana and serves on the OMS board of directors.

Stan Mckim was also one of the first to volunteer for the crusade that had recently begun in Hong Kong. He recalls that:

> Not long after I arrived in the British colony, I met a university student in one of our meetings. His first words to me were "I will believe," and then he added, "I understand, I believe, I want to be saved." On the last night of the special youth evangelistic effort in Ieta, I noticed the same young man and a friend listening very intently and from time to time repeating some English words. After I finished preaching, I talked with them. I can't remember all that we discussed but our conversation climaxed when both boys expressed their determination to be saved. Now began the vital follow-up ministry of training, instructing, and guiding these young babes in Christ. In the few weeks of the youth crusade, we saw hundreds of young people come to church for the first time, and in every meeting we saw victories for Christ and the salvation of souls.

One of the Hong Kong crusaders, Charles McNelly, gained notoriety for one of the most unfortunate accidents to ever befall any of our missionaries. That day he and his Chinese teammates were walking along the narrow dikes that separate the flooded rice fields of Asia. It was raining hard and he had his umbrella up which restricted his view, making it exceedingly difficult to negotiate the narrow footpaths. In the corner of many of these rice fields are large open cisterns which hold fertilizer for the fields, consisting entirely of human excrement. For centuries this has been the primary means of enriching soil in many parts of Asia. The cistern was filled to the brim, and Charles, walking along the slippery dike, was rapidly approaching it and—you guessed it—as he strode forward, the mud gave way under his feet, and he fell head first into the cistern. What happened next we leave to your imagination. He was rescued by an alert teammate and, in a manner not fully described, spirited back to crusade headquarters.

McKnelly's ministry in Hong Kong was greatly blessed. He later wrote:

> Since the beginning of March, we have seen nearly 100 saved. A few days ago, the Lord showed us some wonderful results of the past weeks of labor. We set a date for the beginning of the first probation class. The purpose of this class was to prepare these new Christians for baptism and church membership. How our hearts rejoiced when we began the service that evening. Our little chapel was filled and, when we asked for those who were ready for baptism to come forward, 20 new Christians made their way to the front.

In later years, Charles devoted his ministry in the island colony to the rescue of street boys.

Chapter 22

INTO TAIWAN

Lowell Williamson, who joined the second crusade in 1952, demonstrated commendable managerial gifts. His good judgment and experience were soon recognized by our missionaries in Japan. He remembers that "after a year in Japan, Bud Kilbourne, our field leader, asked to see me. We chatted a bit and then he dropped a bomb shell. 'Lowell,' he said, 'in Formosa (Taiwan) they want to begin the Every Creature Crusade, and the mission has decided that you are the one who should spearhead that work.'"

Lowell had been born in Japan and felt a special call to return to the land of his birth. He reasoned to himself:

Certainly, this must be a mistake. I hardly knew where Taiwan was. In my mind I promptly decided this was not for me. I would decline the offer, but I felt it was a necessary courtesy to say I would at least pray about it. That evening I knelt by my bed, Bible in hand. The Scripture fell open to the Book of Acts. I looked down and, as if in bold letters, I read the words, "Arise and go to the south." I was stunned. I knew Taiwan was indeed south of Japan. I struggled over the matter for two weeks but finally yielded to what I was now convinced was God's will for me.

Lowell received a warm welcome in Formosa, Portuguese for beautiful and the name foreigners used for Taiwan at that time. The field director was Harry Woods, a veteran missionary of the first crusade in Japan and the last OMSer to exit Communist China in 1951. The crusade team in Taiwan was assigned to Ping Tung, a large city in the southern part of the leaf-shaped island. God blessed with gracious fruit and a lively church was founded. In 1954 Lowell returned to Asbury College to complete his BA degree and then enrolled in Western Evangelical Seminary for his Master of Divinity degree. Upon graduation Lowell with his wife, Naomi, returned to Taiwan, taught for years in the seminary, and was elected both president of the seminary and OMS field director. He later also directed the OMS ministry in Hong Kong and mainland China. His son Rodney has followed in his father's train, and today he and his wife Beth are the mission leaders in Taiwan.

I (EE) arrived in Taiwan to continue the crusade ministry which Lowell had initiated. For many years on the field, we enjoyed the privilege of having the Williamsons not only as our beloved co-workers but also neighbors.

Williamson arrives in Taiwan

Williamson and Taiwan team

*Florence Munroe
(Auntie Mun) preaching*

Hong Kong open-air crusade at H Blocks

*Gospel tracts for
Hong Kong refugees*

Hong Kong street meeting

Erny with interpreters, Daniel Chang and Bill Yang, English class

Taiwan funeral mourners in sackcloth

Taiwan funeral

Hong Kong Field Director
Dale McClain

Members of the Washington Club

Erny, street preaching, Tou Liu, Taiwan

Taiwan OMS seminary students, missionaries, and faculty – 1957

Ed Erny, Joseph Wang, and Taiwan crusade team

Erny "riding" water buffalo

Crusade congregation, Yuan Lin, Taiwan

Erny, team lunch

Erny and team, after-service snack

Hong Kong H Block evangelism

Crusader reunion at Indiana Wesleyan Univ. (L-R): Amos, Edwards, Dyer, Schultz, Dupree, Williamson - 2004

Chapter 23

THE ENGLISH HARVEST

Most of the crusaders early on discovered the magical attraction of the English language. Those who attended our (EE) evening meetings pled with us to start English language instruction. Most of the youth, we learned, were far more eager to study English conversation with an American than to learn about Jesus Christ. Today on many OMS mission fields the teaching of English is being used as a powerful means of making friends and drawing people to the church for the very first time. Often these friendships bloom and hearts open to the blessed Gospel. It is a fact that many of Asia's greatest Christian leaders found Christ in and through an English Bible class.

In Taiwan I led my first crusade in the city of Yuan Lin. Things were not going well. This city is famous as one of the best farmland areas in all of Taiwan. It is particularly well known for its luscious fruit and gorgeous roses that bloom in the dark earth. As we labored there week after week, the fertile rich physical soil seemed to mock the fact that the spiritual soil of this strong Buddhist area was anything but fertile. We spent extended periods of time each morning in earnest prayer, asking that God would give us some encouragement and, at least, a kind of first fruit that we could view as the beginning of a harvest in that area. Nothing seemed to happen. In the evening service, we had mostly children or wandering street people who came in out of curiosity and often left early. This was downright depressing.

After some weeks, I finally yielded to my teammates' insistence that I must teach at least one English class. I was dubious that any good would ever come from this effort. I somehow had never really learned English grammar well, a fact that I was usually too embarrassed to mention. We scheduled our first English class for the following Wednesday and we fashioned a sign in Chinese and English placing it by the front door. It read: "English classes taught by Mr. Erny, an American, every afternoon at 3 p.m." American—that was the magic word. Chinese youth wanted to study proper spoken English from a native speaker and also were eager to make friends with foreigners. At three o'clock that Wednesday afternoon, I came downstairs from our sleeping quarters dubious that there would be more than a handful of students for my class. To my utter amazement, the little Gospel hall was packed out. And more than packed out. There were almost as many standing out in the street trying to get in as were actually in the hall. My teammates were patiently introducing themselves and registering the crowd for the first class. We really had no suitable material to use or a textbook other than a New Testament in King James English. Nevertheless, we made a start. My initial efforts as an English teacher were laughable and I was doubtful that any good could come from my feeble, inept attempts. But, despite the many dropouts, we made warm acquaintances with about 20 young people. A number put their faith in Jesus, and some of them remain friends to this day, 50 years later.

It was our custom to give these new converts Christian names since so many of them were studying English. Within a short time the following young men had come to Christ and began attending church:

John, a sergeant in the Chinese Nationalist army, had left family and loved ones on the mainland at age 15. "I'm lonely," he said in broken English. "You know I feel that I want someone to love me." He soon found the lover of his soul.

James, working in a nearby army hospital, said, "I have never been able to understand how to become a Christian. I tried many times but failed. Now I've discovered the way of gladness." He seldom came to services without bringing a friend with him. As a result of his witness, even some of the doctors in the local hospital found Christ.

Peter, who had come to our Gospel hall to learn English, also received Christ as Savior. "Now I understand," he told me with a radiant smile. "God is my father and I am His child. I am reading my Bible two hours every day."

When Mr. Chiu first came to our Gospel hall, he brought a small image of Buddha, saying, "Mr. Erny, I want to present you with my god. He will take care of you while you are away from home in a strange land." I assured him that I had a marvelous God to take care of me. Mr. Chiu came every night to hear about the true God.

Mr. Lin's wife was a Christian lady and had been praying for him for 20 years. With his conversion began the recovery of a life long wasted, void of pleasures, and full of selfishness.

Joseph and Peter were two fine high school boys whom we had been praying with for over a month. They found the Lord and now study the word in their home. Praise God. These are just the first fruits, beginning of God's fulfillment of a promise.

After class one day a young man by the name of Chang (the commonest surname in the world, exceeding in number even the name Muhammed) wanted to talk with me. As we walked through the market place, Chang, a college freshman and English major, began to open his heart to me. He started out abruptly with the words, "I have decided to become a Christian." I could hardly believe what I was hearing. Then he added, "Yes, I have been searching all my life for the truth and I have found it in Jesus Christ. I want you to baptize me." This sounded like a line from a simple missionary drama I'd heard in Sunday school. I felt certain that the young man was yielding to a questionable impulse and probably had no idea the implications of being baptized. He then began to tell me his story:

> I come from one of the wealthiest families in town and also one of the most influential. My father (now deceased) was mayor of Yuan Lin. We have a large home and own much property in the city. I have done well in school and am a good student enrolled in one of the top universities in Taipei, the capital city. But with all that we have had, our wealth, our esteem and our exalted place in society, there is one thing that we have never had in our family and that is true peace and happiness. There is continual infighting, jealousies, and hatred within the clan. Especially intense is the hatred between wives and concubines and the virtual war that exists between the legitimate offspring and the children of concubines. Now I have discovered that Jesus can give peace. He is indeed the son of God and I have put my faith in Him and I want you to baptize me.

This confession left me stunned. I paused a moment for I knew that Christian converts in Buddhist families were often turned out and almost always persecuted. I said, "Daniel (for this is the Christian name I gave him), are you prepared to face the persecution that will come from your family when you reject your ancestral faith?" He said, "Yes, I have thought about that and I'm willing even to die because I know that Jesus is indeed the true God."

Some time later Daniel and his cousin, also an English student whom we named Ruth, were baptized with other believers who had found the Lord there in Yuan Lin. Daniel then began to systematically bring members of his family to Christ. Ruth's father, Daniel's uncle, who had been an alcoholic most of his life was wonderfully saved. Daniel's brother and sister also became believers, shining examples of Christian faith. His younger brother, Stephen, started an English language school in Yuan Lin which over the years has had thousands of students, every one of them hearing the Gospel in the classes. His cousin Ruth enrolled in the OMS Bible Seminary in Taichung and is now a devout and gifted professor in this same school.

Some years later Daniel told me that most of his immediate family had accepted Christ as Savior and were attending the church in Yuan Lin or elsewhere. There were two major exceptions, however; first, his old grandmother, now by tradition the head of the clan, adamantly rejected Christianity. She had worshipped ancestors and idols for 80 years and viewed herself as the spiritual head of the family and even had a large Buddhist shrine in the home. Several years later, however, an amazing thing happened. Grandmother Chang took ill and found that she was dying. She had never before allowed Daniel to share the Gospel with her but now she called for him. "Come talk to me about Jesus," she said. "I am afraid to die." He then proceeded to tell her of Christ and the wonderful salvation that takes away fear of death and gives us joy because He has promised to be with us and give us a home in heaven. She eagerly prayed the sinner's prayer and her glowing face bore eloquent witness to her new faith. A few months later she died and, in accord with her desire, Daniel arranged a Christian funeral and burial for her.

The remaining intransigent member of this family was Daniel's older brother. As the first born, he was typically indulged. He had become a rascal and wastrel who loved to gamble and squandered much of the family wealth. Every time Daniel tried to share the Gospel with him, he ridiculed him and ordered him to "shut up." He had no interest in the Christian faith. Some 20 years later, this elder brother was stricken with throat cancer, probably the result of heavy smoking and chewing betel nut. As he lay on his hospital bed, he found it impossible to speak. All he could do was listen and this he was very willing to do. He realized now that he was approaching the dark doorway of death. For the first time he was actually eager to hear the Gospel he had so long rejected. Daniel visited him and shared patiently and lovingly God's plan of salvation. That afternoon this long-time enemy, the older brother, the head of the clan, was gloriously saved. I had the privilege of preaching at his funeral which was attended by a good portion of the wealthy and upper class population of Yuan Lin.

When we returned to Taiwan in 1964, after I had married and completed seminary, I invited Daniel to assist us as an interpreter in our seminary and also teach English. He eventually joined with me in founding an English language school in Taichung. For more than 20 years we had hundreds of students attending these classes. Part of the instruction was simply English pronunciation and word usage but one third of all the time was always devoted to the study of the Bible and the plan of salvation. Many of those students, including the leading Mormon in Taichung, found Christ as Savior.

Daniel gave up his engagement to a beautiful Buddhist girl and married Carol, the daughter of Mr. Chen, our seminary dean. This distinguished man was an outstanding scholar who had grown bitter after the untimely death of his son. He told us, "I hated God, I raged against God. I shook my fist at God." But through the witness of his daughter Carol, destined to be Daniel's wife, the entire family came to Christ. Another upshot of this blessed friendship with Daniel and Carol was the Chung Tai English Broadcast, an English instruction and Gospel radio program aired six days a week on major stations all over Taiwan for about 20 years.

Daniel and Carol have three outstanding children; all of them know and love Christ deeply. Today their daughter, Amy, plays cello, second chair in the Toledo, Ohio, Symphony Orchestra. Their son, Curtis, is an outstanding Christian doctor, now employed by Eli Lilly Pharmaceutical Company of Indianapolis. Curtis has become a leading voice for Christian medical ethics and speaks in conferences in the United States and abroad. Their youngest daughter, Grace, is married to a former OMS missionary, Tim Heebner. After working and teaching in the U.S., Tim, Grace and their three children have returned to Taiwan where they are on the staff of an international Christian school.

All of this incredible drama was orchestrated by the Holy Spirit, a fact that to this day is totally confounding to me. It was as though God had prepared this great clan of Chinese, representing the largest family on earth, to be His instruments in dispensing the blessed Gospel to their people. Today Daniel and Carol, in their mid-70s, remain active and able soul winners. They also have become well known for their marriage counseling seminars. Daniel is the boldest witness that I have ever known and shares the Gospel without apology with everyone he meets. He has been

God's instrument in bringing great numbers of Chinese into the kingdom. All of this for me is tremendously humbling. My only part was a small one, to listen to God's voice and at first to very reluctantly answer the call to go to a land which I had never seen, to a town I had never heard of, to teach a pitiful English class, and to somehow make known to those dear students the old, old story of salvation.

Chapter 24

HAITI

In 1957 OMS, under the leadership of Eugene Erny, took over the work of G.T. Bustin in Haiti. This small western half of what had once been the famous and prized isle of Hispaniola is peopled largely by former African slaves and is now the poorest country in the Northwest Hemisphere. Bustin had erected a large and powerful radio tower and named his ministry 4VEH, The Evangelical Voice of Haiti. In 1957 he approached OMS about the possibility of taking over the radio station. OMS agreed although the equipment and facilities were now run down and the very costly transmitter in need of replacement. Great labor and expense were required to restore the station to its former effectiveness. In this we were greatly assisted by Men for Missions. With the new radio ministry came some excellent missionaries and national workers, most importantly one of the founding couples, Mardy and Rachel Picasso. Their knowledge of the island and ministry, as well as the Creole language, proved invaluable.

The first missionary assigned to the Haiti Every Creature Crusade was Helmut Markeli from Canada. Helmut was a recent refugee from East Germany. Born during World War II, Helmut's father, a shoemaker, was drafted into Hitler's army and went missing in action. Hence Helmut never knew his father. He finally managed to evade border guards and flee to West Germany and from there to Canada.

In Toronto Helmut found a job in construction. He was accosted by a fellow worker, a bold Christian, who asked three questions:

"Do you believe in God? Do you believe in heaven and hell? Do you know where you are going?" These questions lodged like firebrands in his soul. Day and night, Helmut pondered them. "I was in torment," he recalls. "I had heard a voice as though God Himself was speaking to me and said, 'You are free. I died for you.'" This eventually led to Helmut's salvation. Though Helmut has never acquired great fluency in the English language, he applied to OMS for a two-year assignment as a crusader to Haiti. There he worked with nationals going literally from hut to hut, distributing God's Word in the Creole language and holding evangelistic meetings. In time he fell in love with a fellow missionary, Tina Schwanke. They later were assigned to Indonesia and worked on that field many years until their retirement in 2004.

During the second Every Creature Crusade, altogether some 30 young men from America, the British Isles and Canada volunteered for the program. Of that number, over half became foreign missionaries and the remainder with one or two exceptions invested their lives in the pastorate, evangelism or Christian education.

Chapter 25

THE VALUE OF IT ALL

In the history of OMS, there has never been another program comparable to the Every Creature Crusade for the effective recruiting of young men. In the early 1970s some difficulties arose which for a time quelled the initial enthusiasm for ECC. In a sense the program became a victim of its own success. In the early years numerous teams of nationals and missionary crusaders were planting churches on the average of one every six weeks. These infant churches soon found it hard to both rent a church building and support a pastor. The churches of Asia were still quite poor. Our denominational leaders now found themselves with scores of new congregations, unable to support themselves, thus a financial liability. For a period of time it was agreed that ECC teams would return to the earlier church plants and assist them in evangelism, church growth and programs of Christian education. Now, without the regular door-to-door Gospel distribution, the foreign crusaders' role was no longer viable. Crusaders were encouraged to acquire seminary training, return to the field, learn the language, and become career missionaries. This, many of them did.

In 2001 because the word "crusade" produces misunderstanding and resentment in Muslim countries, the program has been renamed "Every Community for Christ," thus retaining the familiar initials ECC.

Today OMS has nearly 300 ECC teams in Asia, Latin America and Europe. However, they consist entirely of national participants with no resumption of the two-year assignment for crusaders from Western countries which formerly was the most effective recruiting program for new missionaries. Most of these numerous 300 crusade teams are now supported by the generous endowment of the Stanley Tam Fund under OMS direction.

At present, a new program entitled Xtreme Walk is recruiting young men from colleges and churches throughout the English-speaking world. The original vision of reaching every home in a nation has, for the time being at least, been discontinued. Today most of these participants in the new ECC should not be confused with the early crusaders whose energetic focus was to very literally reach every person in the nation with the Gospel

For those of us who had a part in the second crusade (1952-1965), there were joys and rewards beyond measure. Many of us name those years as, "next to salvation, the most important spiritual experience of my life." The campaigns were not, however, without times of great trials and testings. Added to the usual misfortunes of accident and sickness was the fact that all of us were young men with very little ministry experience. Barely out of college, and unmarried, some of us were now separated from sweethearts and fiancées for a two-year period. Also we lived under exceedingly primitive conditions among a people with whom we could hardly communicate. All of these factors combined, at times, to exacerbate some of the usual discomforts and human difficulties.

Six of the young men in that second crusade were engaged when they went to the field. Most postponed their marriages for two years or more. For them, a source of both encouragement and loneliness was to focus on the blessed day when they would return to the homeland and their waiting sweethearts.

For a few, however, the outcome of this long separation was far from what they had hoped for and dreamed of. One of our number who was engaged when he joined the crusade discovered, to his chagrin, that in his absence his loved one's affections had been transferred to someone else. This, of course, was devastating news. It sent him temporarily into depression. He wrote to me in Taiwan of this disaster. I had recently been reading the life of Hudson Taylor, the founder of the China Inland Mission, and had come across the following couplet which ministered to me following my decision to answer God's call and leave Rachel for two and a half years. I sent him the brief verse which has for over a century assuaged the sorrow and grief of many.

> It is enough my heavenly Father knows,
> Nothing this faith can dim.
> He gives the very best to those
> Who leave the choice with Him.

Returning to seminary, Taylor's words were literally fulfilled for my friend. He met and married a lovely and devout young lady from Pennsylvania. They returned to Japan and served the Lord for many years. He will tell you, "I lost the campus queen but God gave me Miss Universe!"

A full century after Charles Cowman and E.A. Kilbourne launched the first crusade (The Great Village Campaign), it would be well to assess the contributions of that program, not only to OMS but to other missions as well. Research reveals that the OMS ECC endeavor has been the model for similar efforts by other missions. The present day Every Home Campaign essentially seeks to do exactly what was accomplished in the initial OMS crusades. ECC was also the inspiration for another ongoing campaign which seeks to put Bibles in every home. The architect of this strategy is Rochunga Pudiate whose organization is called Bibles For The World.

As for the effect of the two-year crusades on the fields, it is instructive to learn that the efforts of those early crusaders continue to bear fruit both in their personal lives and that of their own families. We asked some of the crusaders to state their estimation of the value of the ECC in their own lives.

One OMS leader said, "As our crusade team moved from town to town and witnessed the salvation of hundreds and the planting of scores of churches, it was this more than anything else that drew many of us back to those fields as career missionaries."

From Stanley Dyer: "I need to say that due to the wonderful blessings and triumphs of the crusade, as well as some of the memorable trials and disappointments, many of us have returned to the field and have become missionaries for a lifetime, career missionaries. The Every Creature Crusade had a tremendous influence on me in that, among other things, it introduced me to the Japanese language. This required total immersion in the language and culture. As we worked, prayed and lived with our Japanese teammates day after day, we acquired a vital foundation for future language acquisition. Later when I took formal language training, I had a distinct advantage. In a sense I had already become wedded to the land, the people, the culture, and the language."

It was Hudson Hess's work in the remote mountains of Japan that convinced him of the importance of missionary radio. He has devoted much of his life to radio evangelism through 4VEH in Haiti.

Billy Campbell states, "My two years in Hong Kong in 1965 without a doubt set the course of my life. I was to be a missionary. God had called me. This year I will be 72 years of age, and I have just begun a special assignment as a regional ECC shepherd for Asia. What a privilege, what unparalleled joy to daily glorify God by sharing the Gospel, making disciples and planting churches that multiply among the nations.

J.B. Crouse, reflecting on his two crusade years in Korea, says, "What if I had said no to God's call to be a crusader, to go to Korea for that initial task, an assignment that stretched out over 60 years of service? I would likely never have married Bette, my helpmate in every sense of the word and, more than this, I would have missed the opportunity of being involved in the greatest work of all, fulfilling the great commission."

Duane Beals says, "It is impossible to briefly state how my life has been affected by my crusade experience: travel around the world, learning a foreign language and culture, planting churches, and learning to be obedient to the Holy Spirit. In a broader sense, the sum total of those crusade experiences have made me the person that I am today—a professor in the classroom and a pastor in the pulpit on Sunday and, in a sense, a life-time missionary. The crusade moved me beyond my limited provincial outlook, forcing me to become a world Christian. I have been on the OMS board of trustees for 19 years. In every church I have pastored, we have had a strong mission emphasis. I always urge youth to take advantage of the opportunity to travel overseas to various mission fields while they are still students. When I heard Dale McClain's crusade challenge in that spring of 1962, I had no idea what was in store for me."

Kelly Toth says, "When I came to the end of my crusade experience, I realized that my life's perspective had been eternally altered. I could do nothing less than offer my life to Him for fulltime Christian service."

Buddy Gaines agrees that "it was through the Every Creature Crusade ministry God called me to be a missionary, first with OMS and then later with Evangelism Explosion in Asia and Eurasia."

The value of the ECC in my own life (EE) is of somewhat a different nature. I had been born into a missionary family, son of the president of OMS, and lived most of my life in that congenial and precious environment known as the missionary family. I cannot remember any time in my life when I did not want to be a missionary. Often for MKs, it is not a question of being willing to be a missionary but rather being willing to consider any vocation other than foreign missions. For me, the crisis was accepting God's time table rather than my own.

So the fruit of both OMS crusades lives on not only in the multiplied thousands who received Christ as Savior but also in the hearts and lives of the crusaders, their families, and descendents yet unborn.

OTHER BOOKS BY ED ERNY

NO GUARANTEE BUT GOD
With Esther Erny
Brief biographies of the founders of The Oriental Missionary Society—converted Western Union executives, Charles Cowman and Ernest Kilbourne; Lettie Cowman, famed author of *Streams in the Desert*; Juji Nakada, dynamic Japanese pastor and evangelist.

THE STORY BEHIND *STREAMS IN THE DESERT*
The diary of Lettie Cowman for the year 1924, the final year of husband Charles' life, provides a window into the crucible of physical pain and emotional and spiritual turmoil from which emerged the classic devotional S*treams in the Desert*, destined to bless millions of sufferers.

THIS ONE THING
The biography of missionary leader and statesman, Eugene Erny, a member of the famed Asbury College Missionary team, who held evangelistic meetings throughout Asia in 1929-30. In China he met, courted and won the hand of a young missionary with The Oriental Missionary Society, Esther Helsby. Together they served in China and India until 1950 when Eugene was elected president of the mission, a position he held until 1969.

NOBIE
Nobie Pope Sivley with Ed Erny
A life begun in shame and remorse finds beautiful fulfillment as a young lady travels from West Texas to the remote waterways of Colombia, South America, to offer healing and the message of salvation.

UNDER THE SENTENCE OF DEATH
Valetta Steel with Ed Erny
The epic story of a young pastor, Henry Steel, who upon learning that he is dying of Hodgkin's disease, determines to give himself unreservedly to reaching the nations for Jesus Christ.

THRICE THROUGH THE VALLEY
Valetta Steel with Ed Erny
Valetta Steel, widow of Henry Steel (*Under the Sentence of Death*), tells of the series of tragedies which bereft her of her entire family, testing her faith to the limits of human endurance but also leading to unprecedented joy and fruitfulness.

YIPPEE IN MY SOUL
Margaret Bonnette with Ed Erny

An adventuresome young woman determined to live life to the hilt, Margaret was once engaged to three men at the same time! Later, with her beloved husband's death, she finds her dreams shattered and her life empty. Her search for God eventuates in a life-changing encounter and a date with destiny as God's healer in the remote mountains of Haiti.

HE GOES BEFORE THEM
Meredith and Christine Helsby with Ed Erny and Carroll Hunt Rader

A young missionary family caught in the cross currents of war find themselves Japanese prisoners of war in China during World War II. A moving story of God's miracle provision and quiet courage in the darkest days of the 20th century.

THE QUEST
A small booklet explaining in simple language what one needs to do to be a Christian. More than 100,000 copies in print, *The Quest* has also been translated into a number of foreign languages.

THE KEY GOOSE (And Other Lessons God Taught Me)
Mildred Rice with Ed Erny

Rich spiritual lessons seasoned with humor, gleaned from a lifetime of missionary service in China, Japan and Taiwan.

PRINCESS IN THE KINGDOM
Evelyn Bellande with Ed Erny

Born into a wealthy, aristocratic Haitian family, a young lady finds her dreams broken by a failed marriage and the dark diagnosis of cancer. In her despair, she discovers life and a mission to her own people.

"LORD, THIS IS NOT WHAT I HAD IN MIND
A series of essays detailing humorous and embarrassing episodes in the lives of missionary families.

WHAT NOW, LORD?
Margaret Brabon with Ed Erny

The story of Harold and Margaret Brabon who helped pioneer the work of The Oriental Missionary Society in Colombia, South America, during the dangerous years of "La Violencia." This is a true romance in which a beautiful, idealistic college coed, engaged to a ministerial student, improbably falls in love with a brilliant young chemist working for Henry Ford.

TO INDIA WITH LOVE
Esther Close with Ed Erny
The story of an intrepid missionary nurse in the villages of India.

LEGACIES OF FAITH, VOLUME I, II, III, IV, AND V
Daily devotional readings from great Christian authors, arranged by subject matter and indexed for the benefit of pastors, evangelists, teachers, and Christian workers.

UNDER HIS WINGS
Mary Payseur with Ed Erny
The story of a North Carolina farm girl called of God to serve as a missionary in China where she was imprisoned during World War II.

IN THE DAY OF TROUBLE
Flora Chen with Ed Erny
The courageous story of a Christian woman caught in the horrors of three wars.

MISSIONARY MAVERICK
Elmer Kilbourne with Ed Erny
The incredible and moving story of Elmer Kilbourne, grandson of OMS founder Ernest Kilbourne. Instrumental in helping found World Vision, he also established scores of institutions of mercy following the Korean War. In India he was greatly used of God in the building of more than 200 churches and the founding of Bible schools and seminaries.

YOUNG MEN OF THE CROSS
Ed Erny
The story of OMS' campaign to place the Gospel message in every home in Japan and the ten young men from God's Bible School who assited.